Neon Knight Forever

Neon Knight Forever

The Legacy of Joel Schumacher's Batman Duology

Tomasz Żaglewski

BLOOMSBURY ACADEMIC
NEW YORK • LONDON • OXFORD • NEW DELHI • SYDNEY

BLOOMSBURY ACADEMIC
Bloomsbury Publishing Inc, 1385 Broadway, New York, NY 10018, USA
Bloomsbury Publishing Plc, 50 Bedford Square, London, WC1B 3DP, UK
Bloomsbury Publishing Ireland, 29 Earlsfort Terrace, Dublin 2, D02 AY28, Ireland

BLOOMSBURY, BLOOMSBURY ACADEMIC and the Diana logo
are trademarks of Bloomsbury Publishing Plc

First published in the United States of America 2024
Paperback edition published 2025

Copyright © Tomasz Żaglewski, 2024

For legal purposes the Acknowledgments on pp. viii–ix constitute an extension of this copyright page.

Cover design: Eleanor Rose
Cover image: A still from *Batman Forever*, 1995, dir. Joel Schumacher
© Collection Christophel / Warner Bros / ArenaPAL

All rights reserved. No part of this publication may be: i) reproduced or transmitted in any form, electronic or mechanical, including photocopying, recording or by means of any information storage or retrieval system without prior permission in writing from the publishers; or ii) used or reproduced in any way for the training, development or operation of artificial intelligence (AI) technologies, including generative AI technologies. The rights holders expressly reserve this publication from the text and data mining exception as per Article 4(3) of the Digital Single Market Directive (EU) 2019/790.

Bloomsbury Publishing Inc does not have any control over, or responsibility for, any third-party websites referred to or in this book. All internet addresses given in this book were correct at the time of going to press. The author and publisher regret any inconvenience caused if addresses have changed or sites have ceased to exist, but can accept no responsibility for any such changes.

A catalog record for this book is available from the Library of Congress.

Library of Congress Cataloging-in-Publication Data
Names: Zaglewski, Tomasz, author.
Title: Neon Knight forever : the legacy of Joel Schumacher's Batman duology / Tomasz Zaglewski.
Description: New York : Bloomsbury Academic, 2024. | Includes bibliographical references and index.
Identifiers: LCCN 2023020702 (print) | LCCN 2023020703 (ebook) | ISBN 9798765100608 (hardback) | ISBN 9798765100615 (paperback) | ISBN 9798765100578 (epub) | ISBN 9798765100585 (pdf) | ISBN 9798765100592 (ebook other)
Subjects: LCSH: Batman films–History and criticism. | Batman forever (Motion picture) | Batman & Robin (Motion picture : 1997) | Schumacher, Joel, 1939-2020–Criticism and interpretation. | Superhero films–History and criticism. | LCGFT: Film criticism.
Classification: LCC PN1995.9.B34 Z34 2024 (print) | LCC PN1995.9.B34 (ebook) | DDC 791.43/75–dc23/eng/20230802
LC record available at https://lccn.loc.gov/2023020702
LC ebook record available at https://lccn.loc.gov/2023020703

ISBN:	HB:	979-8-7651-0060-8
	PB:	979-8-7651-0061-5
	ePDF:	979-8-7651-0058-5
	eBook:	979-8-7651-0057-8

Typeset by Integra Software Services Pvt. Ltd.

For product safety related questions contact productsafety@bloomsbury.com.

To find out more about our authors and books visit www.bloomsbury.com and sign up for our newsletters.

For my Bat-family and all the Bat-people out there who still proudly have Bat-credit cards in their pockets

"Dressing like your sister
Living like a tart
They don't know what you're doing
Babe, it must be art
You're a headache, in a suitcase
You're a star"
U2, "Hold Me, Thrill Me, Kiss Me, Kill Me" from "Batman Forever. Music From The Motion Picture"

"It's my Gotham City, and if I want Batman to have nipples, he's going to have nipples!"

Joel Schumacher

Contents

Acknowledgments	viii
Introduction or "Can I persuade you to take a sandwich with you, sir?"	1
1 The Neon Knight begins: The Not-So-Dark Knight as an element in Batman's transmedia multiverse	17
1.1 Into the Bat-verse: From the multiverse of stories to the multiverse of readings	17
1.2 Camp Knight, Dad Knight, or Cute Knight?: Exploring the foundations of the Neon Knight	32
2 The Neon Knight unchained: Questionable choices and the ice-catching spectacle in *Batman Forever* and *Batman & Robin*	47
2.1 "Who's afraid of the big, black bat?": Joel Schumacher as a cinematic trespasser	47
2.2 Tim Burton's Noir-tmare before Christmas vs. Joel Schumacher's camp noir: Embracing a living comic book as a visual thriller	60
2.3 The Lite Knight rises: The troublesome case of plastic figures, virtual grappling hooks, and rubber nipples	77
3 The Neon Knight triumphant: Modern perceptions of Joel Schumacher's Batman duology	107
3.1 "It's so bad, it's almost good": Fandom's online discourse after Joel Schumacher's passing	107
3.2 "Schumacher was right": Social media appreciation for the Neon Knight	116
Closing remarks or "We're going to need a bigger cave"	131
Bibliography	137
Index	140

Acknowledgments

I have always loved the Batman character but I have never truly enjoyed Batman as Dark Knight. Some may see it as quite a weird way to start a Batman-centered monograph, but for me it is the crowning of the years of being a Batman fan—a fan of a very specific Batman. As with most Bat-enthusiasts out there in their thirties and forties right now, I started my Bat-related escapade with the original Tim Burton 1989 blockbuster as experienced through countless VHS replays: the very first truly conscious movie experience of my life. However, with the 1995 *Batman Forever* and its sequel from 1997, a different kind of Batmania had its impact on me. I can clearly remember seeing *Batman Forever* as my very first Batman feature in cinema in September 1995 with my dad. It was an awe-inspiring cinematic spectacle screened in a local movie theater called *Przedwiośnie* in my hometown of Płock—an average Polish city—which for two hours become a neon-laden and quite maniacal vision of Gotham City populated by extravagant characters. I really embraced this bizarre take on Batman's universe although even then it struck me as radically different than the more stoic version delivered by Burton. For years and decades I have tried to cultivate privately this memory of Schumacher's constantly mocked vision-come-true, and now this volume finally becomes my opportunity to articulate my thoughts about that curious Neon Knight and its constantly suspended presence in the conceptual space "in-between": too campy for the "serious" Batman lovers and too serious for the followers of the Adam West-based Comedic Crusader.

As this book finally approaches completion I would like to thank the team at Bloomsbury, especially Katie Gallof, Stephanie Grace-Petinos, and Alyssa Jordan, for seeing something valuable in this particular project and helping me pursue this effort to the end. My gratitude is also due to all colleagues at my home institution—the Institute of Cultural Studies at the Adam Mickiewicz University in Poznań—for providing me (invariably) with the necessary organizational support that was substantial for my work with this publication. The process of preparing this manuscript was financially supported by Adam Mickiewicz University's

Acknowledgments

research program, Inicjatywa Doskonałości – Uczelnia Badawcza, for which I'm also deeply grateful. I would like to thank my "secret collaborator" Szymon Nowak, who was the very first reader of this manuscript and was an invaluable source of all initial linguistic revisions. I want to express as well special thanks to all the social media creators and researchers whose work was used in my analysis, especially Neil Rickatson from 1995Batman.com, all the stuff from the following YouTube channels—Superhero Stuff You Should Know, Vee Infuso, Score PN, Channel Pup, Salazar Knight, I Don't Beat Games, ModernGurlz, Cortex Videos—and the administrators and users of the Joel Schumacher-dedicated groups on Facebook, Joel Schumacher Was Right and Joel Schumacher Fan Page.

I owe a very special "thank you" to my mom and dad, who in my earliest childhood prompted and patiently nurtured the process which yielded this particular book, supplying me with countless comic books, VHS tapes, video games, action figures, and cinematic experiences that culminated in the pages that follow. Last but not least I would like thank my wife, my daughter, and my yet-to-be-born son who will come into the world as this book reaches bookstores; it is an ugly truth that every book is written by both the author and their family, who have to bear with the creative process in daily life. I am very grateful for having my own Bat-family on my side, with my own Catwoman, Batgirl, and Robin in the very center.

Finally, I feel the need to thank the protagonist of this publication—the late Joel Schumacher himself—for having fueled my imagination and the spark that has inspired my private interests as well as professional activities of a superhero-centered consumer and academic researcher alike. It is unlikely that he would ever have thought that the very first monograph dedicated to his conception of the Neon Knight would be written by a scholar from a distant Central European country. Still, I hope that he would have enjoyed it as I have scrupulously tried to comprehend and elucidate the essence of his unique and unorthodox foray into the Batman's lore. The following analysis of the Neon Knight is not intended to convince anyone of the superior quality of his motion pictures, but rather to highlight their cultural applicability which does not have to be tied in with an "objectively" accepted artistic greatness. I think Joel Schumacher would have agreed with that statement.

Tomasz Żaglewski,
Poznań, October 26, 2022

Introduction or "Can I persuade you to take a sandwich with you, sir?"

In 2009 Kevin Feige—the *spiritus movens* of the perennially successful Marvel Cinematic Universe and one of the architects behind the modern renaissance of the superhero trend in popular culture—made a meaningful comment concerning the "importance" of Joel Schumacher's second Batman movie (the 1997 *Batman & Robin*), and its contribution to the rise of the Caped Crusader phenomenon in film:

> [*Batman & Robin*] may be the most important comic-book movie ever made. It was so bad that it demanded a new way of doing things. It created the opportunity to do *X-Men* and *Spider-Man*, adaptations that respected the source material and adaptations that were not campy.[1]

This clearly ironic appraisal of Schumacher's second endeavor in the superhero franchise offers at least several interesting insights into the general perception (or misperception) of the peculiar vision of onscreen heroic feature, which materialized in 1997 and two years earlier (with Schumacher's Batman-centric debut in *Batman Forever*). Even though Feige himself deserves credit for envisioning the narrative structures and themes of superhero films since the first *Iron Man* release in 2008, some critical feedback is surely in order to address his patronizing view of *Batman & Robin*'s final form: one that is still appreciated by many and deserves to be redefined today.

However, after almost thirty years since the premiere of Joel Schumacher's first Batman cinematic adventure, it is still difficult to maintain a serious discussion about these features, as for many viewers and critics alike, Schumacher's Bat-films are simply too aesthetically unconventional or conceptually unserious to be compared with modern cases of superhero cinema. The truth is that probably the best depiction of Schumacher's troubling work with the Caped Crusader was given by the director himself and through the words of the mischievous The Riddler in *Batman Forever*, when the supervillain, played by Jim Carrey, enters the hideout of the film's second antagonist Tommy Lee Jones's Harvey "Two-Face" Dent, driven by his split nature (both psychologically and visually), with the following praise for his soon-to-be partner in crime: "I simply love what you've done with the place. Heavy Metal meets House and Garden Splendid! It's so dark and gothic and disgustingly decadent, yet so bright and chipper and conservative! ... Very few people are both a summer and a winter, but ... you pull it off quite nicely." Knowing the final forms of both Schumacher's movies, it is hard not to see here a camouflaged definition of the director's take on both the character and the Batman franchise at the same time, as well as the main point of concern for the majority of Batman fans unwilling to embrace this stylistic hybrid of a post-Tim Burton legacy and this "improper," much brighter, and comedic input.

Putting Joel Schumacher in the footsteps of Burton in June 1993, after the mammoth financial success of Burton's first Batman in 1989 and the much more controversial yet still profitable *Batman Returns* from 1992, may be seen today as a nonsensical move for the Warner Brothers studio as the new director clearly abandoned the depressive and gothic (yet critically welcomed) version of Gotham City and moved into the territory of making Batman fun and colorful again, just as in the infamous Adam West television show in 1966. Nevertheless, it is crucial to remember here that by doing so, Schumacher actually realized the studios' main mandate for him to re-energize the series into proper blockbuster-like family entertainment after the concerns of the 1992 *Batman Returns* (the 1995 release had gained over $52 million at the American box office and a record-breaking three-day opening with a total worldwide haul of $336,529,144). This also gave Schumacher the opportunity to explore new territory for the comic book avenger in his very own taste and style. And perhaps this personal take is the very thing that makes this discussion about Joel Schumacher's Batman so troublesome to maintain, as until now there was really a very limited interest in trying to understand what the director was actually trying to do with Batman and his mythology.

This book will try to fill that void (and hopefully won't be "naive but insightful" like Dr. Chase Meridian's own work, crudely reviewed in that way by Batman in *Batman Forever*). The best place to start is to consider the striking contrast in the elements that Schumacher used in his Batman formula: the decadent gothic motives with the optimistic, even humorous view. The difficulties with understanding Joel Schumacher's Batman may be the result of this seemingly impossible combination of extremes—the extremes within an utterly eclectic style and an all-over-the-place tone; the critics' reception (Quentin Curtis from *The Independent* praised Schumacher for being "a better storyteller than Burton" and "hit[ting] on a more consistent house acting style, half-way between cartoon and realism"[2] while Gene Siskel complained that *Batman & Robin* was "a sniggering, exhausting, overproduced extravaganza that has virtually all of the humanity pounded out of it in the name of an endless parade of stunt sequences"[3]); competitive financial revenues (the impressive gross of *Batman Forever* was challenged by the financial underperformance of 1997s *Batman & Robin* with its final $238,207,122 global result); and filmgoers' unbalanced memory about these films, unfairly focusing on the nitpicked visual details (like the "scandalous" nipples on Batman's costume) and not the actual meaning of Schumacher's duology. This is why it is essential to finally rediscover these films in the context of a modern superhero renaissance in the media and understand their original structure as well as their surprising legacy, which becomes more and more visible in specific film projects today. There are at least two major points in Kevin Feige's statement (from the beginning of the chapter) that require a radical redefinition given the technically and artistically changing landscape of superhero-based entertainment as well as the newly rediscovered need for the largest superhero-centered conglomerates to address a wide range of aesthetical, cultural, and/or political patterns which can be integrated in these fantastic superhero narratives. As odd as it may sound at this point, the legacy of Joel Schumacher's personal and peculiar touch on the Batman character still casts a long shadow, reaching the most financially successful or critically acclaimed recent superhero releases, such as the big-budget blockbuster of 2022 *Thor: Love & Thunder* directed by Taika Waititi or films like Cathy Yan's *Birds of Prey or the Fantabulous Emancipation of One Harley Quinn* from 2019, somewhat more economically modest yet much more ambitious in terms of the encoded concepts. The first thing that should be asserted in response to Feige's comments about the role of Schumacher's vision is that the "new way of doing things" had actually come full circle over the years and, apparently, returned to the extravagant modality which was once—in the early 2000s—treated as a misguided strategy of making superhero adventures "campy" (both visually and/or thematically). It is quite unfortunate that Sam Raimi's *Spider-Man* from 2002 is actually mentioned as an un-campy feature alongside Bryan Singer's much more down-to-earth and serious treatment of *X-Men* (2000), especially since today it is genuinely hard not to look at Raimi's effort as a direct continuation of the "campy" wave of superhero cinema with just a slightly more realistic tone than the one proposed in the disparaged *Batman & Robin* feature.

Another element from Feige's statement which deserves a response here is as difficult as it is compelling to unpack since it involves less visible qualities and clearly subjective reflections about one's notions of "good" or "bad" interpretation as well as "right" or "wrong" approach towards a given character or the overall concept of superhero narratives, their themes, tone and finally its visual form. In just a few short sentences, Kevin Feige delivers an almost ideal summary of the general understanding of Joel Schumacher's Batman films by encapsulating all these common assumptions into a single, straightforward phrase: "It was so bad." It is not difficult to imagine the most popular opinions or beliefs one could gather in a public survey on the contemporary reception of *Batman Forever* and *Batman & Robin*. People would mention the infamous "rubber nipples," cite inferior one-liners and silly catchphrases provided by the absurdly cartoony villains, discuss the dominance of style over substance, the not-so-ambiguous gay subtext, the essential lack of some serious tones in the story, etc. In other words, one would discover that basically the Schumacher movies do not evince the "right" approach towards the Batman character nor do they epitomize the "right" idea of superhero cinema in general. However, Joel Schumacher's Batman duology is a perfect and insufficiently explored case study for cultural research, an opportunity to examine the use of "right" and "wrong" arguments with respect to single-superhero-oriented texts and the strategies of employing either adjective in the changing context of time, the evolving perception of superhero movies, as well as the constantly growing inventory of modern features, in terms of which Schumacher's perspective may still be viewed as desirable or unwelcome by specific audiences.

This is the case with the aforementioned *Thor: Love and Thunder* produced by Marvel Studios, which met something of a backlash from fans and critics for being too "Schumacher-like" in terms of its aesthetic aspect and the disrespectful portrayal of the main character. In an article posted on Movieweb.com, tellingly titled "Is *Thor: Love and Thunder* the MCU's *Batman & Robin*," the author Richard Fink makes a few observations about the most obvious parallels between Waititi's and Schumacher's movies: they represent the fourth installments in the ongoing franchise, use the conjunction "and" in the title, and portray the main antagonist as "a central villain who is motivated by a loved one's tragic ending but where both villains eventually realize the errors of their way and finding their humanity."[4] Still, the text formulates several more detailed assumptions and accusations that establish a seemingly tight artistic link between *Thor: Love and Thunder* and *Batman & Robin* as a means of direct critique, which it may be worthwhile to quote more extensively:

> Both *Batman & Robin* and *Thor: Love and Thunder* were highly anticipated sequels before their releases, and each had huge opening weekends. Yet word of mouth from audiences and critics was less kind. A common complaint about both films is that they essentially double down on what made the previous film work without providing anything different. ... *Thor: Love and Thunder* increased the comedy of *Thor: Ragnarok*, with more jokes often giving the vibe of a sketch comedy or an improv group tying together the plot (which makes sense, considering just how much improvisation went on during production). However, the comedy clashes with the source material that the film is adapting, primarily the dark Gorr the God Butcher story and Jane Foster's Mighty Thor storylines from the comics, which are a much more serious affair. ... Aside from both being the fourth solo film for a superhero and being the sequel to a course correction entry, another interesting element both films share is a strange tonal balance. *Batman & Robin* and *Thor: Love and Thunder* both focus on comedic elements while also featuring a major character suffering a life-threatening disease which clashes with the overall tone. ... A film can juggle a variety of tones, but it does become hard to take the more dramatic moments seriously when the rest of the film has been winking and trying to make the audience laugh

throughout. In *Batman & Robin*, the subplot of Alfred dying feels at odds with the throwback nature toward the 1960s series, while in *Thor: Love and Thunder* the cancer storyline seems disconnected from both the loose comedy and the dark main villain, and feels worthy of a story on its own.[5]

To sum up Fink's concerns, the crucial elements include "joking up," which apparently constitutes an unwanted approach to Marvel's God of Thunder and DC's Dark Knight, as well as the stylistically and thematically convoluted storylines which rely on over-the-top humor and more serious topics in a manner that is impossible to reconcile—according to the article at least—and prevents either from easily being either comedy or drama (since an effort to achieve a hybrid form is supposedly distressing to the viewer's perception). In the broad discourse concerning *Thor: Love and Thunder*, Fink's text is no exception—especially in social media content such as memes, gifs, or YouTube comments—which soon after the premiere iterated the critical narrative about the disproportionate mixture of laughs and drama, as well as echoing the overtly negative reception of Waititi's vision of Thor, whom many fans actually found to become a character to laugh at, not laugh with. Exemplifying such a response is a meme posted on a Facebook group called I F****** Love Films, TV and Theatre on July 9, 2022 by one of the users. The graphic collage featured four movie posters—from the 2018 *Thor Ragnarok* directed by Taika Waititi; *Thor: Love and Thunder*; *Batman Forever*; and *Batman & Robin*—with a rather direct commentary: "*Thor: Ragnarok* is like *Batman Forever* … being different from the first 2 installments by adding more color & humor for a decent balance making it very entertaining. *Thor: Love & Thunder* is like *Batman & Robin* … going so ridiculously overboard with the humor & craziness that it ruined the characters & the movie itself."[6]

It is obvious then that Joel Schumacher's legacy of Batman movies is still exploited as a negative reference to certain modern films that—just like the Schumacher features—"erroneously" head towards frivolous depictions of their characters (or even the entire storyworlds in fact) or upset the acceptable hierarchy of both comedy and drama by amplifying either (or both) to such an unbalanced degree that the originally unrealistic and quite cartoony characters become … too cartoony. Nonetheless, it would be unfair to highlight only the mocked aspect of Schumacher's presence in superhero discourse today, since recent years have seen a new wave of appreciation for his aesthetic taste and personal interpretation of Batman lore gains more and more enthusiasts among real-life and online social groups. The movement grew substantially more conspicuous and vocal in 2021 following the promise of a so-called *Schumacher's Cut*—a significantly longer (approximately 170 minutes) and apparently more director-oriented original version of *Batman Forever* which was semi-officially announced by Akiva Goldsman, the screenwriter of both Joel Schumacher's *Batman* flicks. Goldsman himself tried to hype up the potential release:

> By the way, *Batman Forever* still has a renaissance coming. I really am interested to see whether the original cut of *Batman Forever* comes out because I got to see it, recently, the very first one, which was Preview Cut: One. It was really dark, it was a pretty psychological exploration of guilt and shame. ... I have it on pretty good authority that there exists in the Warner Bros. vault a 170-minute cut of *Batman Forever*. I think that it went much deeper into his [Bruce Wayne's] childhood psychosis and his mental blocks and that it was a more serious, darker version of that movie that was one of the first assemblies that Joel filed with the studio and they eventually cut it down because they were like "it's too dark for kids. We gotta sell these Happy Meals, so maybe let's not invest ourselves in the trauma of childhood murder. We've got Jim Carrey, let him do some s—t".[7]

As strange as this idea of a "dark and serious" version of *Batman Forever* may sound for those critics whose reception of Schumacher's work still revolves around its being "fun and campy," the preview of *Schumacher's Cut* in 2021 rekindled public attention in that particular version of Batman in the wake of Joel Schumacher's passing on June 22, 2020. One could say that this renewed interest for the once easily-ridiculed *Batman Forever* may have stemmed from Goldsman's assurance of the film having been "fixed," specifically by bringing back the "darkness" into the Dark Knight's 1995 story and giving the audience the "proper" Batman—the brooding vigilante who constitutes the quintessential image of that particular character. Despite the possibility that the "final" *Batman Forever* would move away from its original form and the enduring imagery of Schumacher's Batman, various media reports in 2021 noted growing interest in *Schumacher's Cut* as another likely case of delivering an author-oriented vision of a film following popular demand, right after the efforts of the *#ReleaseTheSnyderCut* Twitter movement culminated in releasing *Zack Snyder's Justice League* in 2021.

A global social media event to support the *#ReleaseTheSchumacherCut* campaign was launched on June 16, 2021 on Twitter. As of June 2023, the official Twitter account dedicated to this project had gained over ten thousand followers and became the space of constant celebration of Joel Schumacher's Batman legacy, as users tenaciously petitioned Warner Bros. Studios executives to have them officially release *Batman Forever*'s extended version. The Twitter account has also shared lots of Schumacher-related content with the community, including fan-made merchandise, Batman-related memorabilia, Schumacher's private appreciation posts and favorites images, and scenes and memories from the generally infamous "nippled era" of the Gotham City hero's presence onscreen. Just as with *Zack Snyder's Justice League*, the leading figures of the *#ReleaseTheSchumacherCut* community entertained the same hope that the unseen material would become available through Warner's streaming platform services or standalone Blu-ray/DVD editions, whose fan-designed covers and collector's boxes circulated widely in associated social media accounts and profiles. Perhaps the most notable achievement associated with the still-prospective extended feature is not the film itself but the gradual social recovery process which is quite palpable in today's perception of Joel Schumacher's Batman movies—a recovery that in fact involves a revival of interest in this still widely controversial and rejected idea of a superhero's portrayal deriving from a single author's strong personal vision. As Anthony Lund perversely asks in his remarks about the *#ReleaseTheSchumacherCut* trend:

> Ever since Warner Bros. seemingly gave into demand, bowed down to fans and released the fabled Snyder Cut of *Justice League*, many have taken this to mean that creating enough noise on social media can get the same reaction for any movie. Whether the decision to release Zack Snyder's version of the DC blockbuster was truly down to fan power or was the plan all along is something that will probably never be entirely known, but that won't stop

fans of the 90s Dark Knight offering of *Batman Forever* joining together on 16th June to demand Joel Schumacher's first cut of the movie be released in the form of—wait for it—*The Schumacher Cut*. Well, who saw that name coming?[8]

The recent resurgence of Joel Schumacher's Batman can surely be seen in online activities and the growing public awareness of the features once rejected for being "too silly" or "too colorful"; also, it makes minor yet quite meaningful attempts to become once again a fully accepted part of the officially supported canon of Batman mythology. In *Detective Comics* no. 1052, published in February 2022, the regular readers of Batman comics faced a rather unexpected cameo appearance of a secondary character from Schumacher's Dark Knight film features. In the sixth part of a story entitled *The Tower*, written by Mariko Tamaki and illustrated by Max Raynor, the opening scene presented Batman fans with an easily identifiable depiction of a young blonde woman in a doctor's gown hanging from a large antenna shaped like a question mark. Although the setting was a little rearranged, it was an obvious nod to the perils of Dr. Chase Meridian, played in Schumacher's *Batman Forever* by the Australian actress Nicole Kidman, who had been in similar plight in the finale of her blockbuster debut. Following Mariko Tamaki's narrative, the readers discovered that that female protagonist was in fact a comic book incarnation of the earlier cinematic heroine, with minor alterations to the original character design. In this new iteration, Tamaki's Dr. Meridian was not Batman's love interest as such but a girlfriend of the villainous The Riddler's former fiancée, who dumped the criminal for Chase. Despite all the necessary updates, the very fact that a mainstream comic book storyline actually reused a seemingly expendable figure from a widely disregarded cinematic work may be seen as yet another indication that elements originating from Schumacher are reclaimed into Batman mythology and may be "canonized" through artistic decisions and fan reception alike. It seems that the residues of both *Batman Forever* and *Batman & Robin* are now penetrating into this acceptable space of thematic and aesthetic overhaul as presented in *Detective Comics* no. 1052, whereby the films' legacies are built upon with a modern twist and sensitivity. According to a reviewer from CBR.com, this refurbished image of the psychiatrist portrayed by Nicole Kidman certainly meets some of the expectations regarding the relationship between the character and the then version of Batman—played in 1995 by Val Kilmer—due to the need for a more nuanced interaction. The review states:

> By recreating *Batman Forever*, the comic brings the character back to her movie origins and makes it clear that there is not and never will be any romantic connection between her and the Dark Knight, even when he saves her life. ... *Batman Forever*'s final choice between Meridian and Robin was a defining moment for that cinematic pairing between her and the Dark Knight and established their romantic relationship. By redefining the motivations between the two in that scene, as well as giving Chase Meridian another, totally separate love interest for it too, it makes it definitively clear that this is not the character from the 1995 movie. This is a modern version of Dr. Chase Meridian for a modern age and she is the one who defines her own character, not Batman.[9]

However, the most likely welcome return of specific characters from Schumacher's Batman era is not the only noteworthy element in the "renaissance" of public interest in those movies asserted by Akiva Goldsman, as considerable numbers of modern memorabilia and exclusive gadgets yield increasing profits, sustaining the market with Schumacher-related items for his fans. Toy producers, manufacturers of action figures, and suppliers of exclusive collectibles have recognized that there is a sound financial logic to relaunching merchandise connected directly with *Batman Forever* and/or *Batman & Robin*. In recent years, the growing legion of Schumacher enthusiasts were able to buy a set of Funko Pop figures, including all the main characters from the Schumacher-directed Batman movies and even rare variant editions, such as The Riddler—all covered in green and question marks—in the Funko Pop Artist Series or Mr. Freeze's glow in the dark limited edition figurine produced originally for the 2020 Funko Summer Convention. The Funko series was accompanied by other "cute" items, such as Hot Toys Cosbaby Two-Pack Set including Batman and Robin, re-envisioned in their "adorable" variety. Yet another line, scheduled to launch in September 2023, is Iron Studio's Mini Co PVC statues, of Val Kilmer's Batman, Chris O'Donnell's Robin, and Jim Carrey's The Riddler. Vehicle enthusiasts may purchase metal die-cast and highly detailed models of the iconic Hans Rudolf Giger-inspired, quasi-organic Batmobile from *Batman Forever* by Jada Toys in two different scales: 1:24 with a plastic figure of Kilmer's Dark Knight or a smaller 1:32 item. For the more demanding and affluent collectors, Hot Wheels trumped Jada Toys with an even bigger Bat-car in 1:18 scale and a plethora of additional features: a lighting mode that made the metallic car much more true-to-screen with its neon-like glow which brought back the unadulterated, original appearance of a flashy Batmobile from the third cinematic adventure of the 1989–97 era. Still, the absolute must-haves for the most discerning consumers were delivered by superior memorabilia and figure creators Hot Toys Limited and Prime 1 Studio, who revealed their extremely polished forms of *Batman Forever*-based statues of Batman's "Sonar Suite" from the movie's third act and Robin's original costume (both by Hot Toys) as well as fandom's much-appreciated "Panther Suit" as worn by Val Kilmer for a substantial amount of his screen time as Batman (by Prime 1 Studio).

These highly expensive and equally desirable art objects—as these masterfully designed items can legitimately be called—premiered in spring 2023 and it would be reasonable to assume that even the exorbitant price (approximately $255 for the Hot Toys take and over $1,500 for the Prime 1 Studio's figure) will not deter the most devoted fans, who have patiently looked forward to such impressively made recreations from their childhood. The creator of the YouTube channel Justin's Collection—dedicated to reviews and commentaries on all media-related merchandise—admitted in his video report on the Hot Toys premiere that "even though the movie is a little bit campy and a little bit wacky I grew up watching this film on repeat on VHS so it does hold a special place in my heart and thank goodness Hot Toys decided to solicit these figures."[10]

This Introduction opened with a meaningful quote from Kevin Feige concerning the overall status of *Batman & Robin* (and perhaps also *Batman Forever*), which arguably constitutes the direct opposite of all "good," "acceptable," or "contemporary" standards espoused today by filmmakers, superhero fans, and professional critics interested in the Caped Crusader in whichever multimedia format he may appear. The thing that needs to be underscored here—at the very beginning of a book dedicated exclusively to Joel

Schumacher's contribution to the superhero formula, erroneously understood as no longer relevant—is that the paradigm of approaching Schumacher's Batman in a never-ending contrast to all other superhero features is in no way efficient, fair, or acceptable today. The core issue in discussing Schumacher movies is that since the very premieres of *Batman Forever* and *Batman & Robin* they have been invariably talked about with "diminishing contrast" to other Batman pictures or superhero films in general. It is argued that those pictures are not as "gothic" as Tim Burton's versions of the Dark Knight, not as "realistic and serious" as the more recently acclaimed Christopher Nolan's Dark Knight Trilogy, not as "entertaining and universally pleasing" as the regular installments of the Marvel Cinematic Universe, or that they are "totally campy and outrageously silly" like Adam West's Batman, and so on.

When looking at Schumacher's creations by way of contrast to the other (apparently more successful or accurate) reifications of Batman or other heroic cinematic depictions we may lose sight of the essential and still-unresolved question that one needs to ask: "What is Joel Schumacher's *Batman* duology really like?" I do believe that, over a quarter of a century after the premiere of *Batman Forever*, regular cinemagoers or even professional cinema researchers are still not sufficiently interested enough to engage with those bizarre yet fascinating cinematic experiments which have so much going for them in terms of artistic and cultural patterns. The necessity for such an examination—as I elucidate in the following chapters—is more pressing than ever given previously noted social media interest and possible financial profits; the inevitable conclusion is that people increasingly realize that Joel Schumacher's films are way more complex than befits merely a poor, older cousin of today's blockbusters.

Although the main goal of this book has already been stated, it is still necessary to clarify what it is and is not about. First of all, its primary focus is on Joel Schumacher's Batman films in terms of their contemporary relevance and attractiveness, with the presumption that they constitute original and unorthodox conceptualizations of the superhero figure onscreen. Attention will then be drawn to certain behind-the-scenes details of Schumacher's work as well as the indispensable context of him becoming the director of Batman movies, including an overview of his previous achievements and cinematic portfolio. However, one should not expect the following chapters to provide a comprehensive study of Schumacher's filmography, since this would inevitably call for a separate and much more broader scope, going beyond the Batman-related associations and parallels. The main concern here is to elucidate Schumacher's very own interpretation of Batman by means of the figure of the Neon Knight—a rival category capable of describing Batman's characteristics alongside other commonly known designations such as the Dark Knight, Camp Knight, or Cute Knight.

The first part of this book will unfold an origin story, so as to situate the Neon Knight concept within the vast realm of territories occupied by other Knights, which make up a truly impressive cultural, artistic, and political multiverse accrued from different incarnations of what is nominally a stable persona. Subsequently, the book will go on to examine Schumacher's approach to Batman in the light of certain principal categories which continue to inform criticism of that particular concept. In Chapter 2, section 2.2 will explore the "living comic book" category—responsible for the Neon Knight's final appearance—as it fueled Schumacher's vision of the superhero cinema as a living cartoon: replete with bright colors, highly aestheticized imagery, and excessive visual and musical trappings. A further section will address the debate on the Batman content originating with Schumacher, which revolves around three different concerns about his impact on Batman's legacy: the "toyetic" nature of Schumacher-driven Bat-franchise, abortive "gamification" efforts which produced a number of Schumacher-styled game titles, and, finally, the director's alleged personal inclination to "not understand" the Batman character, manifesting in enhanced sexual overtones in his features, namely the appalling presence of bat-nipples in the center of the hero's costume. The goal is to approach those issues from today's perspective—without the initial outrage prevalent in the 1990s media and the barely nascent online feedback—to determine whether the notion that Schumacher was "wrong" in this treatment of Batman and that he essentially failed to understand the source graphic material "correctly" is still warranted. In the third, and final, chapter I will advance an observation that may be absolutely crucial in these deliberations. Bearing the categories of "cultural memory" and the key role of online communities and digital discourse concerning

Schumacher's legacy in mind, one must examine the most recent views regarding the phenomenon discussed here from the standpoint of actual taste, sensibility, and—as Svetlana Boym suggested—a "nostalgic bond" (2001) shared by numerous Schumacher fans today. Thus, one can arrive at truly inspiring deductions about the films, perceive how certain allegations or biases change over time, as well as see how the awareness of themes and forms admissible in a superhero narrative evolve. In the closing remarks, I will give voice to Schumacher's enthusiasts and their conceptual efforts to enliven Schumacher-related discourse. I will therefore highlight all the values and qualities which a substantial group of Batman fans found meaningful, citing various excerpts from online discussions and recent colloquy from which "appreciation" discourse gradually emerged.

The subtitle of this introduction is the opening line delivered by Batman's loyal butler and friend Alfred (played by Michael Gough) in the first few minutes of *Batman Forever*. Over the years, that particular quote has become a single-sentenced symbol for all that is "Schumacher-like" in the Batman's mythos—feeble humor and an all-too-conspicuous suggestion of a merchandise-oriented narrative backbone that few failed to notice in both Schumacher films. It feels right to start this exploration of Schumacher's legacy with those particular words, not just because they are the first words one will hear in his first Bat-film, but because it is necessary to confront the two principal assumptions regarding Schumacher's approach—its thematic silliness and shallow commercial motive. However, the intention of this book is not to convince everyone to look at Schumacher's films as "deep," "serious," or "socially relevant;" instead it will attempt another effort: to explain why exactly—despite all the extravagance and ostentation—those productions deserve a fresh look for being one of the most non-standard and unique versions of a superhero character ever put onscreen. The "tragedy" of the underappreciation of Schumacher's duology lies in its enduring "in-betweenness": they are too unorthodox and too bizarre to become general crowd-pleasers whilst being too commercially driven and mainstream to be inducted among underground cult classics. Nevertheless this peculiar limbo is a major indication that Schumacher's vision sought to venture into spaces that basically no other cinematic incarnations of Batman have ever been interested in entering. It may be encapsulated in one single enigma—and the mother of all Batman-related riddles—which describes the main aspiration of Schumacher's efforts: Why is Batman forever? Therefore, Alfred's question seems apposite once again, since prior to unlocking Batman's forever status one may grab a snack before my analysis starts to unfold, or—to paraphrase the opening scene from the 1995 *Batman Forever* yet again—it may be necessary to take a drive-thru somewhere along the way.

Notes

1 Devin Meenan, "Why Kevin Feige Thinks Batman & Robin Is One of the Most Important Comic Book Movies Ever Made," Slashfilm.com, March 9, 2022, https://www.slashfilm.com/793647/why-kevin-feige-thinks-batman-robin-is-one-of-the-most-important-comic-book-movies-ever-made/.

2 Quentin Curtis, "Wholly boring, Batman!," Independent.co.uk, July 15, 1995, https://www.independent.co.uk/arts-entertainment/cinema-wholly-boring-batman-1591745.html.

3 Gene Siskel, "No.4 'Batman' Strikes Out," Chicagotribune.com, June 20, 1997, https://www.chicagotribune.com/news/ct-xpm-1997-06-20-9706200276-story.html.

4 Richard Fink, "Is Thor: Love and Thunder the MCU's Batman & Robin?," Movieweb.com, July 17, 2022, https://movieweb.com/is-thor-love-and-thunder-failure-mcu-batman-and-robin/.

5 Ibid.

6 I F**king Love Films, TV and Theatre, Facebook, July 9, 2022, https://www.facebook.com/photo/?fbid=2638197456314944&set=gm.2055872464600814&idorvanity=593788057475936.

7 Neeraj Chand, "Batman Forever Writer Has Seen #ReleaseTheSchumacherCut, Says a Renaissance Is Coming," Movieweb.com, May 6, 2021, https://movieweb.com/batman-forever-the-schumacher-cut-exists-akiva-goldsman/.

8 Anthony Lund, "Batman Forever Fans Plan #ReleaseTheSchumacherCut Trending Event for Next Week," Movieweb.com, June 8, 2021, https://movieweb.com/batman-forever-release-the-schumacher-cut-trending-event/.

9   Andrew Herbison, "Detective Comics Just Recreated Batman Forever with One Big Difference," CBR.com, February 12, 2022, https://www.cbr.com/detective-comics-recreate-batman-forever-difference/.

10 Justin's Collection, "Hot Toys Batman & Robin from batman Forever – Figure Preview Episode 83," YouTube, 2021, https://www.youtube.com/watch?v=l9lCrKNlr_0&list=PLvOhZIQVv6hBvq8nIHmaVMfZP0ya5a0i7&index=32.

1

The Neon Knight begins: The Not-So-Dark Knight as an element in Batman's transmedia multiverse

1.1 Into the Bat-verse: From the multiverse of stories to the multiverse of readings

The cover of *Detective Comics* no. 241 from March 1957 could have a regular Batman stories reader seriously astonished. The drawing created by the artist involved in the issue, Sheldon Moldoff, was a rather peculiar depiction of the Dark Knight, wearing an aggressively red—almost pink in fact—bat costume and looking at a whole collection of other multicolored outfits: in shades of green, yellow, or orange. The cover itself invited a possibly stunned reader to a storyline entitled *The Rainbow Batman* and announced by a brief dialogue between the Pink-ish Knight and his faithful companion Robin: "'But, Batman, last night you wore the green costume—and tonight you're wearing the red! Why?' asked Boy Wonder and his companion responded: 'I must, Robin—I must wear a different-colored Batman costume each night!'" The story itself, written by Edmond Hamilton, represents a classic case of what one could call "typical" Batman text from the 1950s narrative vault, dominated by heart-warming depictions of Batman's fellowship with Robin and virtually sensation-free entertainment. Hamilton then introduces The Boy Wonder during his normal superhero duties, as he escapes from the scene of a robbery and ends up injuring himself. In the subsequent part of the story, the young acrobat continues his search for criminals accompanied by Batman, who begins to don increasingly brighter and colorful suits for his everyday patrols. In the conclusion to this quite bizarre Batman adventure, it is explained that the Dark Knight's strange new preference for a rainbow wardrobe stem from his concern for the boy's fate and the risk of Robin's alter ego—Dick Grayson—being recognized due to the child's visible injury. Although the story itself is not really interested in commenting on those new iterations of the Dark Knight, who successively becomes the Red Knight, Yellow Knight, Green Knight, or Orange Knight, nor does it seek to insinuate some possible changes in the standard depiction of the "dark" attributes, such as loneliness, grittiness, or aggressiveness, it is actually a compelling cognitive exercise in "Batmanology" to imagine how differently the Orange Knight could act and solve criminal cases without the staple "broodiness" evoked by the equally standard outfit of black and gray.

The idea of asking for a pastel depiction of Batman in comics or any other media may seem like blasphemy to the majority of his fans, on a par with the demand to make a film about the deadly Xenomorphs from the 1979 Ridley Scott's horror classic that follows the pattern of a romantic comedy instead of the unconditionally expected tale of gore and blood. One may ask, however, if the process of un-darkening the Dark Knight—both visually and thematically—can really hurt the hero so deeply that he will no longer be a relevant character. And it is not as if the conundrum has only just arisen—over the decades since Batman's debut in 1939, there have been distinct movements or currents which challenged the generally accepted "darkness" of the Dark Knight due to changing political and/or social climates, the fluctuating interest of the readers and creators, and the necessity of reimagining Batman to match new ages and trends. The orthodox supporters of the one and only acceptable as well as the most "original" version of the truly dark Dark Knight may thus find it difficult to defend their position, as from the very beginning of Batman's existence in the comic book form the period of time when the character actually remained in line with the stock image of a lone vigilante was in fact quite brief. Just a few months after Batman's first appearance, the shadowy hero gained his most iconic companion in the person of Robin, The Boy Wonder created by Bob Kane, Bill Finger, and Jerry Robinson for *Detective Comics* no. 38 of April 1940. Invoking Bob Kane himself, Will Brooker observes that

> The introduction of Robin ... changed the entire tone of the Batman stories. Robin lightened up the mood of the strip and he and Batman would engage

in punning and badinage as they defeated their adversaries. The brightness of Robin's costume also served to brighten up the visuals and served as a counterpoint to Batman's somber costume. More significantly, the addition of Robin gave Batman a permanent relationship, someone to care for, and made him into a fatherly big brother rather than a lone avenger.

(2000: 56)

In the 1940s wartime stories and notably in the American Comics Code-regulated superhero narratives of the 1950s and 1960s, Batman stories maintained a rather family-friendly tone and mellow graphics that differed so drastically from the widely presumed seriousness and ferocity that most Batman fans take for granted. It is genuinely interesting that even today such a departure from the gothic image of Batman—so typical of the aforementioned incarnation of the character in the Golden and Silver Age of American comics—is still treated in the general discourse as a mistake rather than a possible variation of this fictional figure. As a result, the otherwise quite informative video-essay posted by YouTube channel Salazar Knight (dedicated to the continuing presence of Batman in comics), in which the author discusses the "troubling" decades of the 1950s and 1960s, was symptomatically titled "Batman's Real Nemesis … The Silver Age,"[1] implying that the stories such as *The Bizarre Batman-Genie* written by Dave Wood and penciled by Sheldon Moldoff for *Detective Comics* no. 322 cannot be treated as equally "real" or "acceptable" incarnations of Batman, given that the imagery of a violent avenger and a wish-fulfilling Caped Crusader in a turban are too remote from each other to involve the same character.

In his famous line from an interview for *Los Angeles Times*, Grant Morrison—one of the principal architects of Batman's modern embodiment in comics—shared a critical formula which ensures permanence and attractiveness to a character that defies the passage of time. The interviewer observes: "I'm fascinated by the flexibility of the character. Batman is a cheery Saturday morning cartoon with 'The Brave and the Bold' but he's also beating people to a pulp in 'The Dark Knight', a film that pushed the limits of PG-13. He's a Fisher Price toy for toddlers and a sociopath in Frank Miller's books. And nobody blinks." Morrison replies thus: "Supple is the word. It's really weird. Batman can take anything. You can do comedy Batman, you can do gay Batman ... it all works. It something intrinsic to the character. It's so strange and amazing."[2] Morrison offers a plain and simple explanation of a very popular characteristic that became almost an indisputable mantra for many Batman scholars and researchers. The key thing here is the idea that a single fictional character is able to accommodate as many different interpretations and incarnations as possible in response to a wide range of audiences and demographic groups which may be interested in drastically different aspects of the same figure. The concept was successfully tested in Batman studies by scholars such as Roberta E. Pearson and William Uricchio (1991) or Will Brooker (2000) in their applications of the "floating signifier" category, derived from Tony Bennett and Janet Woollacott's study of James Bond's similar capacity to adapt to the ever-changing needs and demands of the readers or creators (Bennett and Woollacott 1987). Although there is nothing new in examining fictional characters like Bond or Batman through an analytical effort to identify the so-called "moments of Bond" or "moments of Batman"—i.e., every single and particular use of the character in a specific context of time, politics, and culture—one cannot fail to emphasize the "acceptance" factor affecting certain "moments of Batman" or their validity for particular groups of "users" of the character. In other words, as promising as the "floating signifier" happens to be in superhero study involving Batman and similar figures, it should presume one vital objective, namely account for the aforementioned approval for specific variations and the volatile nature of recognizing certain iterations as "accurate" or at least "tolerable."

The "floating" nature of Batman—construed as a never-ending migration across media, artistic patterns, readers' demographics, and political contexts—turns out to be a fundamentally important matter for all cultural researchers interested in tracing how individual forms of culture are consumed while others are rejected/negotiated. After all, the issue lies at the root of twentieth-century cultural studies, shaped by the University of Birmingham's Centre for Contemporary Cultural Studies in the 1960s with its major figures of Stuart Hall, Angela McRobbie, Paul Williams, David Morley, and John Fiske. The problems previously explored to understand how British viewers actually "comprehended" the encoded message they consumed through television broadcast may still resurface in modern inquiry into accepting or rejecting contemporary media messages, which can also involve the colorful characters of superheroes. With the rise of social media and the growing openness to multiple competitive readings of every single fictional or non-fictional product, character, and service, it has become even more vital to be aware of the diversified notions that may be pushed by various factions of social actors, in favor or against the existing "preferred" version of a particular phenomenon.

This has been very aptly observed by Jennifer Dondero in an essay on modern online fan communities dedicated to the Batman persona and the strategies of "hijacking" official stills or images to make personalized memes and gifs which articulate the dominant or counter-dominant interpretations of the Dark Knight's basic attributes. Dondero adopts a very interesting perspective on comparative research between the "canonical" substance (sustained by the official Batman-related material and subconsciously shared by the general audience) and subjectified "head canons," formulated by individual "users" through all types of independent releases which can adhere to or negotiate with the more universal understanding of the character. The essential element here is that according to Dondero's analysis, the vast majority of "bottom-to-top"-generated representations endorse the classic Dark Knight's dark appearance, even by amplifying Batman's commonly known brutality or phenomenal intelligence to a truly superhuman and absurd level. Dondero explains:

> One of the many memes that highlight this particular aspect of Batman's character is a macro image of a panel from *World's Finest* #153 (November 1965). The image is Batman slapping Robin, and the original text has been replaced with Robin starting to ask Batman what he got his parents for Christmas and Batman yelling, "My Parents are Deeaaaaaaad!" While this meme certainly pokes fun at the art of older comics and Batman's ever-present angst over his parents murder, it is also a sign that Batman fans recognize that, at his core, Batman is motivated by understandable human grief. Canonical material and fans like to revisit the idea of Batman as a hero with a tragic past because it is a human motivation we can all recognize. The fact that Batman perpetually grieves for his family is especially poignant in light of how stoic and detached he forces himself to be in order to be a hero. Consequently, Batman allows himself to be dark, mistrustful, cold, and sometimes highly immoral with regard to his personal relationships. Essentially, he sacrifices the things that make human so he can be

more than human as Batman. This resonates more with fandom than a hero motivated by his own intrinsic goodness.

(2013: 36)

Despite his "floating" abilities and a possible range of adaptation skills to suit many different uses or visions, the Batman character appears to be strongly hunkered in this one single model which seems to eclipse all more unconventional versions. His graphic and thematic incarnations can indeed recycle any genre-dependent patterns or artistic styles—situating Batman in the Victorian age, a Wild West adventure, space exploration alongside his Justice League companions, or future cyberpunk-like exploits—yet all these variants are expected to respect the apparently one and only "true" understanding of Batman as the Dark Knight (both visually and psychologically). As Jeffrey A. Brown rightly notes, Batman constitutes a cultural nexus—a figure that can integrate many competitive readings which span children's TV series in *Batman: The Brave and the Bold* (2008–11) and the psychopathic Zack Snyder's vision in *Batman v Superman: Dawn of Justice* (2016). However, it is tacitly understood that one major iteration represents possibly the most accurate depiction of the character. According to Brown,

> the enduring popularity of *The Dark Knight Returns* has made it a type of *de facto* bible for understanding the character. *The Dark Knight Returns* is still ranked as the best Batman story ever in hundreds of online lists. Moreover, the brooding and resolute persona that Frank Miller solidified for Batman in the mid-1980s remains at the core of the character in most modern depictions. Variations of Batman continue to emerge and find expression but these alternative Batmen always remain on the margins of canonicity.

(2018: 23)

A question arises at this point: what about all those marginal Batmen (and Batwomen) out there, who seek their expression of Batman beyond the 1986 canonized interpretation by Frank Miller? What about all the Knights that want to avoid the "Dark" element or at least aspire to broaden its shared meaning with features or qualities that are uncommon for the traditional Dark Knight, both in terms of his appearance and behavior? Is it even feasible to remain the Dark Knight outside the "darkness" element or, to draw on Jeffrey A. Brown once more, outside the widely espoused Batman Prime embodiment? Is there a textual and cultural place for an Orange Knight and his colorful companions and followers?

The faithful adherents of the canonical Batman concept would argue that the appellation "the Dark Knight" is there for a reason and the very idea of erasing certain "essential" qualities of Batman—like the externally and internally projected "broodiness" or roughness—can simply lead to the erosion of the character itself, resulting in such drastic changes that they may basically undermine the very core of this hero. Still, the real question is whether the multilevel "darkness" component really translates into the independence and attractiveness of Batman as a fictional character, and how much damage would really be caused by imbuing that "dark" representation with somewhat brighter elements. Here, one could refer to the most essential and fundamental characterization of the Batman persona by Jim Beard, summarized as follows:

1. Batman is Bruce Wayne.
2. Bruce Wayne's parents were murdered when he was a boy, inspiring him to become a crimefighter.
3. Bruce Wayne dresses in a bat costume and calls himself Batman to fight crime.
4. Batman's mental and physical powers are at the peak of human capability.
5. Batman is an inventor who has created many devices and vehicles to aid him in his crimefighting.

(2010: 57–8)

In this particular list, the "darkness" or "grittiness" characteristic is conspicuously missing. In other words, one may assume that some factors are even more critical to defining the Batman character than the qualities denoted by the "dark" attribute, whereas removing them still leaves numerous narrative and/or conceptual building blocks to recognize Batman even outside the influential thematic shadow of *Dark Knight Returns*. Batman's "fluid" essence once again inspires diversified optics, as one can easily cite other "substantial" conceptualizations of the Dark Knight in which the "dark" element plays a much more significant role than in Beard's list. This is the case in the greatly influential approach developed by Roberta E. Pearson and William Uricchio in their watershed publication in Batman studies, where both authors also attempted to define the core idea that makes Batman the character he is:

> His name was The Batman. A dark, mysterious character of the night, stalking the streets, defying criminals with intelligence, athletic powers and state of the art gadgetry, terrifying enemies who dare cross his path. The Batman had a secret identity, that of Bruce Wayne, wealthy playboy. At a very young age his parents were killed on the streets of Gotham City …
>
> (Pearson and Uricchio 1991: 183)

By accentuating the role of "night stalking" or "terrifying criminals," Pearson and Uricchio certainly draw on the Dark Knight's most canonical understanding, which nonetheless may be more of a cultural variant than a stable and indisputable paradigm since—as already noted—there are even more essential depictions of Batman's defining attributes without the "dark" component. Moreover, shortly after his graphic debut, the hero created by Bob Kane and Bill Finger gravitated towards less dark narrative patterns, therefore one could theoretically argue that the *Dark Knight Returns* depiction is the anomaly rather than the bright and happy Silver Age Crusader. It all whittles down to earlier Will Brooker's conclusion that the fictional Batman figure requires a specifically cultural approach to the very idea of "authorship"—both in the official products and individual interpretations alike—since the effort to formulate the conclusive and definitive understanding of this hero actually reflects user's own taste, expectations, and experiences of a character instead of bringing out inalienable elements of this fictional creation (see Brooker 2012). The issue is also highlighted by Alex S. Romagnoli and Gian S. Pagnucci:

> What every superhero has is a collection of media over a given number of years that defines who that character is in the sociocultural context. Some heroes have more prominence than others, of course, but the variation in representation of these characters is what constitutes a canon of superhero literature. It is impossible, however, to include any and all representations of one superhero and claim that one superhero represents the entire canon of superhero literature. … Bloom's "aesthetic value" encompasses that which seems most important when reading literature and/or texts of any kind: whether the story sticks with us.
>
> (2013: 192–3)

Once again, the ultimate explanation for the dominance of a given depiction of Batman—namely the Dark Knight—should be considered a strictly cultural as opposed to aesthetic matter in view of its high degree of self-reflexivity and the evidently "floating" aspect of the character itself, with its unstable set of "defining" characteristics or connotations. This is even more important than asking about the premise behind canonizing the Dark Knight and marginalizing the "rainbow" incarnations of Batman, which after all offer a genuinely broad range of possible social or political "uses" of this hero.

As Kevin K. Durand observes in his essay about the "hybrid" nature of Batman's long-standing presence, the quest to define "Batman Prime" or the "dominant" Batman interpretation is ineffective, since it tries to come up with carved-in-stone explanations and impose a hierarchical framework within an organically unstable phenomenon which—as noted earlier—forges its substantial incarnations in response to highly subjective experiences and expectations pinned on the character. All these efforts to designate a selected "Batman Prime" version and then assess all the other variants relative to this core idea merely confine the analytical possibilities within Batman studies as well as produce unfair assumptions that lead to social conflicts consisting in "my Batman is better than yours" arguments. According to Durand, the crux lies in the very nature of the so-called superhero canon and the manner in which it should be understood by fans and scholars alike to fully embrace the "floating" capacity of characters like Batman. Instead of the traditional postulation that traits in a fictional canon are supplied by the official texts, nurtured by creators, as well as safeguarded by curator-like fans who protect its stability and completeness, it may be much more efficient, Durand explains, to alter the notion of a canon's nature towards a much more inclusive and culture-conscious modality called a hybrid canon, which transcends the restrictive terms of the "official" and non-canonical uses. Durand suggests:

> With respect to the question of canonical authority, the strength (and weakness) of any hybrid canon is that no particular instance can claim with much authority that status of authority. This is particularly true with Batman. The canon is so diverse that no particular franchise can claim canonical primacy; while, at the same time, the major moments (of which there are many) can all lay claim to primacy. Thus, for these reasons, we

must answer the opening question of this essay with a resounding, "No, there isn't a definitive Batman; there are, in fact, several."

(2011: 92)

Durand's proposal once again may seem a virtually destructive assumption for the majority of comic book fandom and superhero readers, who have already grown accustomed to the necessity of controlling and gate-keeping the canon in its essence as a "sacred timeline" of narrative which encompasses the "right" versions of heroes and events. Still, it would be interesting to apply Durand's perspective to yet another fundamental term for comic book stories, namely fictional multiverse, which should consistently be approached from the standpoint of cultural acts instead of strictly diegetic patterns. As Andrew Friedenthal explains comprehensively in his study concerning the DC multiverse structure:

> Though the DC Multiverse primarily exists as a setting for narratives, it also exists as a kind of map of the entire imaginary world of DC Comics. By allowing for multiplicity, the multiverse gives creators the ability to continually flesh out the details of this infinitely expansive imaginary world, creating a massive structure within which endless narrative permutations can take place …. It aids the writers, artists, editors, and other creators in maintaining … invention, completeness, and consistency. In regard to invention … the multiverse provides the opportunities for creators to chart and explore worlds that differ from our own in ways that the main DC universe, designed to simulate the world outside our windows (save for the existence of superheroes, magic, aliens, and the like), does not.

(2019: 8)

As a narrative structure, multiverse is an excuse to effect counter-factual and counter-diegetic revisions of certain characters or events within the controlled mainframe of fictional universes of DC or Marvel comics, construed as a self-contained and interconnected set of stories. In Karin Kukkonen's study, this "counter" structure of superhero multiverses triggers interesting options as the multiverse structure can initiate variantization of any given narrative model and, consequently, be an exercise in launching alternative mental models for readers to comprehend and integrate within broader understandings of a specific storyworld (see Kukkonen 2013: 161). One may thus assume that the very existence of a multiverse paradigm is a much welcome opportunity for making the traditionally gate-kept superhero patterns (e.g., the Dark Knight standard) more inclusive and aesthetically malleable, due to the growing potential of envisioning a counter-canonical version of Batman who abandons his Dark Knight roots and transitions towards a lightened appearance. This is the inherent promise of creating a multiverse—finally encompassing a possibly infinite number of readings that align with the expectations of a hybrid canon, and demanding a higher degree of revised and personified uses of "floating signifiers" embodied in superheroes. William Proctor construes multiverse in line with the concept of "forking paths," which was conceived by Jorge Luis Borges, as this layout symbolically describes the notion of multiverse in physics, where quantum mechanics is represented by the eponymous garden of forking paths: "a spatiotemporal labyrinth comprising 'an infinite series of times, in a growing, dizzying network of divergent, convergent and parallel times'" (Proctor 2017: 324). For this study, however, the real concern is how radically revisionist these competitive paths can really be, with the massive conceptual "neutron star" of Dark Knight looming within the multiverse of Batman-related texts and readings.

As Terrence R. Wandtke explains, the logic of revisionism is crucial for superhero readings and readers since—as the author himself notes with respect to Batman—the artistic and economic continuity of the long-lived Caped Crusader's stories in a transmedia environment is shaped by the constant sine wave of competitive understandings of the character, going from one extreme to the other and crossing through multiple possible intermediate stages in between (see Wandtke 2007: 6). This clarifies the cultural and aesthetical aspect of the multiversal model since its very essence is a promise of eliciting as many possible variants and variations as possible—in this case catering to the enthusiast of the grim Dark Knight and a more optimistic, rainbow-themed crusader alike. Outside the strict limitations of the main single timeline or a stock franchise idea, the multiverse offers an opportunity to truly embrace probably the most valid quality of superhero narratives: their neo-oral specificity, a direct upshot of the openness of classical oral culture to radical modifications within the mainframe of a story due to the changing nature of the storytellers and listeners. In *Retcon Game. Retroactive Continuity and the Hyperlinking of America*, Andrew J. Friedenthal highlights the fact that modern culture's thoroughly transmedia mode of producing and consuming any given popular story—via diverse media channels, electronic devices, and online communities—actually sustains this mature form of the "second oral culture," which derives from Walter Ong's original concept of primary and secondary orality, where the former reflects the manner of participating in the storytelling process in traditional cultures as a dialogue between the audience and the content of a story itself (see Friedenthal 2017: 18). The key factor here is the acquiescence to all the necessary repetitions and corrections within the narrative that should be permitted due to the evolving nature of that cultural act, including the shifts in social awareness, historical context, or just simply individual expectations towards a presented fiction. Drawing on the classic insight of Umberto Eco, the trick with superheroes as present-day instances of the oral tradition is to discern this continuing tension between their stable (defined) attributes (the mythic elements) and the much more flexible narrative elements, which can and should be susceptible to a shifting set of qualities that a specific costumed character is supposed to manifest in the eyes of the equally variable array of their actual "users" (see Eco 1972).

This "idealistic" model of multiversal structure and its properties of a fully inclusive and tolerant paradigm is one thing, the actual application of such a strategy is another, especially as it entails much more complicated negotiations between the "acceptable" or "unacceptable" readings or the already mentioned marginalization, since certain "forking paths" are relegated to the narrative fringe. This is prominent in the Batman phenomenon and its enduring reliance on the Dark Knight-centered appearance, which seems resistant to any attempts to "lighten up" the hero and immediately dismisses such efforts as "unofficial" or "uncanonical" readings. This is the case with the famous *Batman* TV series made for the ABC network in 1966—inclusive of its iconic "campy" costume—which, as Richard Reynolds observes in his analysis, was "never intended to form part of the overall Batman DC continuity, and fans have no problem separating these texts from the structure of continuity and enjoying them in isolation from the canonical works" (1992: 43). The key thing, however, is once again to discern this enduring notion that the

Not-So-Dark Knight is a travesty or at least a distant outlier with respect to the core portrayal of the thoroughly Dark Knight, which does not admit any radical changes in tone or form. Alternatively, the un-darkened variants are acceptable in the "mainstream" as long as they enrich the visual patterns but do not affect thematic interpretations since, as Drew Morton argues, "fans appear to have accepted stylization … as an alternative to verisimilitude. However, the limit of the acceptance amongst fans ends where style takes on the negative connotations of camp" (2017: 59). Again, the problem here lies in the strictly hierarchical notion about the "true" representation of Batman and its "secondary" readings, which actually goes against the multiversal nature of superhero stories, in which competitive renditions are equally significant in cultural terms. The "core" Batman can never become an Orange Knight, the "essential" Batman should never demonstrate a more optimistic approach, he is constantly resistant to the happy, trauma-free, and un-darkened persona. Such variations are to be found in the deliberately child-friendly products and media content such as the recent *Batman: The Brave and the Bold* animated show on Cartoon Network or the Lego Batman iteration—the very form and appearance of the minifigure automatically encourages a more permissive approach. Still, is it really such an outrage to embrace other iterations as the "core" reading of Batman? Are the available Rainbow Batmen really unable to add to the character's features, so that it may become the multicultural and multi-aesthetic "floating signifier" which so many scholars and readers are looking for?

Today, one readily observes an ongoing race to have the "multiverse" agenda implemented ubiquitously in corporate products and services—especially those whose franchises and trademarks originate directly from comic book sources. However, the application of the "multiverse" concept appears quite shallow, being nothing more than a slightly broader classic "universe" approach, involving an interconnected strategy of combining distinct movie/comic book series and groups of characters. As yet, the actual ability of the multiverse to delineate separate paths of readings for specific characters is not manifest; the point is not to diversify Batman or Doctor Strange by changing the actors or their garish outfits, but to situate them in a completely different set of narratives, since many "uses" of these heroes can be seen as an admission tickets set in different visual settings, bringing distinct aspects of the characters to the fore. After all, it is not the pre-projected depressive tone or psychological "darkness" that truly makes Batman a timeless phenomenon—this idée fixe could and should be regularly challenged by new and fresh visual and thematic "colors." If "secondary orality" is indeed applicable in superhero analysis, then it should embrace its most fundamental cultural quality, which Terrence R. Wandtke identifies after Walter Ong as the triangulation of the additive, aggregative, and redundant features that have an impact on this phenomenon (see Wandtke 2012: 31). Ultimately, it all leads to a fundamental observation concerning the status of superheroes and their analysis as multiversal characters: their "cores" or "definitive" characteristics cannot be decided by way of hierarchical or apparently "objective" canonical readings, but rather construed as an amalgam of individual experiences, understandings, and expectations towards such figures, which indeed result in certain readings being "canonized" or "de-canonized" in an evolving structure of social and political agendas. Nicholaus Pumphrey observes that "The reader influences the canon and continuity as much as the canon and continuity influences the reader" (2019: 48). Hence, this study should ask why the Orange, Camp, or finally Neon Knight—as competitive readings of the Batman mythos—exist on the margins of the "core" Dark Knight personification and why it would be productive in terms of knowledge yield to bring them out of analytical obscurity.

In a very informative video-essay about Joel Schumacher's *Batman* movies, popular YouTube film reviewer and analyst Patrick H. Willems prefaces his sincere homage to the Schumacher era with an interesting observation:

> I'm at San Diego Comic Con, the nerd mecca of the West. I'm surrounded by an endless, overwhelming display of fandom and what you'll see more than almost anything else here is Batman. Countless versions of Batman. Comic book Batman and Michael Keaton Batman. And Ben Affleck Batman and Adam West Batman. And the Batman Who Laughs and Batman Beyond. And Lego Batman. But there's one Batman you never seem to see. That many people would rather forget.[3]

Naturally, the repressed Batman is Schumacher's, a Batman demoted to a periphery even more distant than those inhabited by the Campy Knight from the 1960s or the Lego Batman, condescendingly regarded as a children's-only character. It would be fair to assume that he is the most outrageously "wrong" and "unwanted" Batman: the most direct and vivid opposite to the central Dark Knight, which in fact should not even be considered admissible within the open multiverse structure. Willems underlines that there is generally no interest in imitating this incarnation even amongst the most Batman-fixated cosplaying fans. Which qualities, then, make this particular vision the worst of all Batmen? How far did Schumacher go in his misunderstanding of who Batman is and how the character should act? Interestingly enough, even during the early showings of Schumacher's first *Batman Forever* there were many voices that identified that particular vision as misguided within the acceptable scope of Batman's interpretation. Andrew Goldman—a journalist for the entertainment news site Vulture—recalled *Batman Forever*'s premiere in an in-depth interview with Joel Schumacher, openly admitting:

> Charlie Rose had a whole segment on *Batman Forever*, the Monday in 1995 after it had the highest-grossing opening weekend in history; with $52.8 million in three-day grosses, Batman Forever unseated previous record holder 1993's *Jurassic Park* ($47 million). Those films now hold the No. 217 and No. 261 spots, respectively, on the list; 2019's *Avengers: Endgame* is currently on top with $357 million. David Denby from *New York*, Janet Maslin from *The Times*, and Stephen Schiff from *The New Yorker* all talked about how bad it was as a film, and for cinema in general. Maslin did concede her children, 6 and 9 years old, enjoyed *Batman Forever*, and Denby remarked, "My 12-year-old loved it and has seen it twice. He thought it was awesome, and we got into a terrible fight." Denby said he thought it was "disgraceful."[4]

Considering the earlier discussion about the conservative nature of Batman's canon and the absence of a genuinely multiversal approach in evaluating all possible readings of the character, Joel Schumacher's Knight and his perception over the years is perhaps the most fascinating, as it is spurned by the fans of Adam West and Michael Keaton in their choices of Comic-Con costumes on the one hand, but, on the other, sees a growing range of *Forever*-based merchandise (as referred to in the Introduction).

Within the hierarchical structure that the Batman-centric transmedia multiverse happens to have, one may assume that the Schumacher-directed Neon Knight would rank in the inferior regions, just below other unconventional Dark Knight readings like the Camp Knight, Lego's Cute Knight, or the quite numerous crowd of the Bright Knights that have inhabited many media over the decades, e.g., the Sunny Knight conceived by Roberta E. Pearson and William Uricchio to describe the Batman fiction in the postwar and Comics Code-regulated DC magazines of the 1950s (see Pearson and Uricchio 1991). The Neon Knight concept rises from that specific line of the Lighter Batmen, with all the inevitable connotations that the Bright Knights generated over the years, including their most pivotal "tendency to a sunnier Batman … identified as not just sunny, but positively gay" (Brooker 2000: 146).

Before moving on to a description of the Neon Knight's features, it may be necessary to delve into this long line-up of pre-Neon Knights, who shared and pursued essentially the same aim of removing the strict conceptual and graphic darkness from the Dark Knight. It would be interesting as well to see whether this "un-darkening" process destroys Batman as a predefined figure or perhaps uncovers some non-traditional facets of the character's significance and socio-political "usefulness." In keeping with this section's principal premise—i.e., the indispensable recognition of Batman's multiversal aspect as a tool of exploring the cosmos of Rainbow Knights which epitomize many parallel readings—it is time to examine a number of such instances as outcomes of campfire-like narratives (see Peretti 2017: 10), which may demonstrate some advantages over the most airtight depiction of the dark-ish Dark Knight.

1.2 Camp Knight, Dad Knight, or Cute Knight?: Exploring the foundations of the Neon Knight

In his explicitly titled article, *Why Batman Movies' Obsession with Realism Hurts The Dark Knight* in 2021, Anthony Borrelli advances a valuable argument concerning the excessive and strongly compulsive striving to embed the hero in the realm of "realistic" stories, as in the acclaimed Christopher Nolan trilogy. Accordingly to Borrelli:

> This Batman gave audiences a taste of what they had been missing in the films more concerned with practicality than theatrics. Unfortunately, this does more harm than good in respect to the Dark Knight's on-screen potential. While realism is great for exploring Batman's inner state, it inadvertently places limitations on the creative aesthetic of the character. All black armored Batman suits are perfectly acceptable and impressive, but it's not the same as seeing Batman in black and gray. Sadly, the black and gray is often one of the first casualties to realism as it's less practical for stealth operations. The same goes for the Batmobile where style is often lost in favor of utility. Part of Batman's appeal is his aesthetic and theatricality, which is not always "practical."[5]

The realization that this so-called "practicality" leads to a more realistic rendition of the Batman character is an interesting addition to the previous discussion about the general reception of the Dark Knight's persona, as it highlights yet another ingredient commonly affirmed by the most orthodox fans—namely heavy reliance on that particular like-in-real-life quality. It is true that over the years Batman has been recognized as the superhero best suited to be presented in this particular manner, one who could be most readily associated with potential vigilante acts taking place in the world outside the reader's or viewer's window. The basic lack of any superhuman abilities, dependence on fantastic but not "practically" inconceivable gadgets and vehicles, as well as the consistently expanding lore of Batman's physical strength and intelligence, the result of long years of training, all seems to call directly for a realistic setting and the presence of a non-supernatural avenger whose deeds bring SWAT operations to mind. Yet another paradox of Batman's creation—as Borrelli aptly argues—is the almost organic hybridity of a character who has to reconcile "practicality" with a significant amount of graphic theatricality resulting from the overly dramatic or even downright cartoonish nature of Batman's superheroic exploits, with a gallery of equally outlandish villains to boot.

The effort to place Batman in a setting of commonly understood realism—a striving for a "verisimilar" depiction of Batman's actions and endeavors or, in other words, their ability to be imagined within the established laws of physical and psychological worlds—can be seen as yet more proof of the Dark Knight's core understanding, whereby the "darkness" connotes "seriousness" so as to automatically preclude any forms of "silliness" that could damage the character's "realistic" vigilante look. This is openly asserted by Mark S. Reinhart in his definitive *The Batman Filmography*, where the author strongly criticizes Joel Schumacher's *Batman & Robin* for being too remote from the limits of the "realistic" approach. As Reinhart puts it:

> But as bad as *Batman & Robin*'s formulaic nature is, the film has even bigger problem—namely, it is completely divorced from any sense of reality. As discussed last chapter, *Batman Forever*'s use of computer graphics technology perhaps gave Schumacher and company *too* much freedom, because it allowed them to stray far beyond the boundaries of what a hero like Batman could do if he were actually a real person. This problem was magnified tenfold in *Batman & Robin*. Characters are flying through the air at impossible speeds and trajectories, cars are being driven over wildly uneven terrain, and roads suddenly dead end right in the middle of bridges that look to be 50 stories off of the ground.
>
> (Reinhart 2013: 187)

This particular section in Reinhart's work describes in detail how Schumacher's films depart from the expected image of the characters and, in fact, identify the entire narrative and aesthetic ecosystem that the more serious nature of these heroes should involve. As regards *Batman & Robin*, Reinhart censures the film's excessively bright and pastel-colored tonality, even more immoderate re-homosexualization of costumes with the notoriously conspicuous rubber nipples, and misguided color palette; finally, there is a garish quality to Gotham City resulting from accentuated "shades of magenta, orange and lime green, and these colours did not seem to match up with the images of the dark, shadow-lined streets of Gotham City" (2013: 188). After a comprehensive critique of the "look" with which Schumacher endowed his Batmen, Reinhart makes a final statement that could serve as an unequivocal apotheosis of the "proper" Dark Knight's portrayal: "This combination of 'non-Batman costumes' and 'non-Batman colours' made *Batman & Robin* feel like a—well, like a 'non-Batman film'" (188).

Even so, Schumacher's films are actually far from being the first to be ostracized for flouting Dark Knight's "dark" look, nor were they the first to be regarded as acts of "softening" the character by avoiding brutalism and tonal grittiness. In the history of the Bat-related Bat-media, the title of the most tonally challenging and pastel-dominated vision still belongs to the classic *Batman* TV show which debuted in 1966, while its Camp Knight became an antecedent to the younger incarnation of the Neon Knight. Chronologically, that particular version was not the first ever attempt to deliver an "un-darkened" idea of Batman (as already observed, Batman comics would consistently lighten the mood right after Robin appeared in the 1940s), but for the regular Batman-consumer Adam West's interpretation remains the most iconic portrayal of a lighter vigilante. Throughout the decades since its first release, the ABC show tended to be associated with the notion of "camp," which the successive film scholars and critics such as Will Brooker, Roberta E. Pearson and William Uricchio, Glen Weldon, and Jeffrey A. Brown repeatedly confirmed, noting that the producer William Dozier often invoked the concept in the sense coined by Susan Sontag: as a serious approach to thematically and visually ridiculous material. Here, however, it is necessary to reconsider the campness of the 1960s *Batman* as a direct opposition to the widely shared notion of the Dark Knight's serious nature. The essential philosophy behind the show was probably summarized most accurately by its head screenwriter and conceptual co-creator contributed to the show's ultimate form, Lorenzo Semple Jr., whose formula was cited in *Batman: A Celebration of The Classic TV Series*, an artbook by Bob Garcia and Joe Desris: "I conceive this whole thing being so gorgeously square that it's hip; so far Out that it's In. No necessity to make it modern by using teenage slang and what not, indeed on the contrary" (Garcia and Desris 2016: 22). Semple Jr.'s words reflect the peculiar nature of the show, simultaneously highlighting the hybrid nature of Batman's rendition—it is steeped in the 1960s visual and tonal style yet it tries to maintain a distanced approach towards the tenet of up-to-dateness by keeping Batman in a tension between countercultural spin and a straight superhero fantasy, good and proper. To sustain such a paradox the show in no way resorts to any sort of "realistic" flavor; on the contrary, it manifests its penchant for radically unrealistic performance and technical execution quite vulgarly. Again, it would be most for fitting to cite one of the 1960s *Batman* main contributors, namely Jack Senter who was the series' art director. The latter stated in Garcia and Desris's artbook: our impromptu Batcave "was exciting to look at, because the true source of it all was a comic book. We wanted credibility, but we didn't want reality" (Garcia and Desris 2016: 28).

The story is pretty much known from that point on. The 1960s *Batman* became a synonym of the unrealistic, comic book-y approach, favoring the appeal of graphic narratives of the Golden and Silver Age, utilizing their pastel, bright, and unrealistic color schemes and introducing equally nonsensical exploits whose noisy timbre amplified the tension. Without doubt, the approach aimed to deliver the Not-So-Dark Knight in visual and psychological terms, as Batman's appearance and behavior would not correspond with the paradigm of a "serious" hero. It was something of an ulterior motive to demonstrate the real possibilities of the newly marketed color TV sets, which is why *Batman* keenly explored all the aesthetic "unrealism" one could achieve at the time by designing the film language of the series and the onscreen exploits using every available film trick, including extensive use of Dutch angles, iconic onomatopoeias, characteristic voiceovers that commented on the events in a manner of narratory blocks in comics, or the extremely pop-art-like effect in character appearance. Costume designer and wardrobe manager Jan Kemp recalls:

> When I received the assignment to work on the *Batman* series, I decided to get every copy of the *Batman* comic books that I could lay my hands on …. I soon realized this project would require a different approach in regard to costumes and I decided to give the actors a vivid combination colors and styles that had not heretofore been used in films or television, and by so doing translate into real life the garish look of the comic-book pages …. The idea being that television (as a medium) was stereotyped and that it could only carry certain colors. I claimed and (was) later proved right that we could use all sorts of "ultra-violent" colors and get away with it.
>
> (Garcia and Desris 2016: 38–9)

Still, one could ask about the actual positive corollaries of juxtaposing that Camp Knight with the much more acceptable appearance of the Dark

Knight. In other words: why exactly should the Camp Knight be as valid as his most "serious" and "realistic" counterpart? Mark S. Reinhart observed in his own appraisal of the 1960s interpretation that the very introduction of that campy character was a crowning act in a much longer-term strategy within the DC Comics, which actually accelerated the process of "softening" the character, initiated in 1940s and successfully continued in the 1950s following Frederic Wertham's critique of the subtextual "gayness" of Batman and Robin's relationship; in conjunction with the alleged taste for violence, it culminated with the infamous Silver Age comic book Knight facing sci-fi themes and dangers: a Martian attack or sudden appearance of a giant ape. William Dozier's *Batman* surely derived from that frivolous understanding of the Caped Crusader; all the same, having intensified the characteristics typical of the Silver Age, it achieved the goal of demonstrating the not-so-obvious advantages of disengaging the Dark Knight from the shadowy realms. According to Will Brooker, the unexpected and still insufficiently appreciated legacy of the 1960s *Batman* consists in the aesthetic alternative to the most common visualization of Batman as a dark figure, waiting in a dark alley for a black-coated crook … in the night. No matter how iconic this image may be to the audience, it certainly does not exhaust the capacity of the graphic imaginings of Batman that work equally well when saturated with more visible or—as Jan Kemp stated—ultra-violent colors that yield less brooding but similarly awe-inspiring images of a superhero in action. The artistic possibilities of portraying Batman's adventures can be readily expanded by making them more graphically abstract or absurd (in a creative and entertaining fashion) than the standard depiction of a gargoyle-like vigilante. Brooker sums it up thus: "An obsessively 'dark' Batman, after all, is potentially flatter than any Pop canvas; to achieve any degree of subtle, rounded shadowing, readers and producers alike may have to accept Batman in his costume of 1968 as well as that of 1986, in his camp as well as his sinister mode, in light as in darkness" (2000: 248). At any rate, the faithful followers of the essential Dark Knight capable of accepting the "camp" stylistics over the years had an even bigger pill to swallow. As Drew Morton suggested, there was yet another aspect of that particular interpretation which, in all likelihood, remains the most problematic aspect of the Camp Knight's legacy: the transformation of a hypermasculine macho ideal into a Bat-dad persona.

The major success of ABC's *Batman* with viewers—on its debut, the show received a phenomenal rating of 27.3/49 from the American audience, as documented by the report of the Nielsen institute[6]—was followed by an equally aggressive and enthusiastic rise of Batmania, evinced in the tremendous volume of Bat-related merchandise and everyday products. The other consequence of the series starring Adam West was growing demand to know more of the Caped Crusader's exploits as the main target audience—children and young teenagers—are certain to have developed Bat-fever in 1966. The show itself ran for three seasons—ending on March 14, 1968—and spawned an iconic cinematic feature directed by Leslie H. Martinson in 1966 and distributed by 20th Century Fox as a direct companion to the hit television production. The William Dozier-inspired iteration of the Camp Knight did managed to continue in other forms of popular media which, albeit not treated as explicitly integrated sets of narratives within the 1966 *Batman* sub-universe, were nevertheless too close to its manifest nature and aesthetic to be treated as something else than semi-official spin-offs.

The first of those was the animated show *The Adventures of Batman*, produced in 1968 by the iconic Filmation studio for the CBS network. The cartoon debuted in the US on September 14, 1968, nearly six months after the last episode of the live-action series. It was made by the Filmation company, who specialized in express production of low-budget cartoons and animated shows in its peak period between 1963 and 1989. Even before *The Adventures of Batman*, the company were known for the rather limited quality of their titles, reflecting the fittingly defined limited animation technique preferred by the studio. Nonetheless, the Filmation studio—founded by Lou Scheimer, Hal Sutherland, and Norm Prescott—managed to create quite an impressive library of characters and popular series over the years, including *The Hardy Boys* (1969–71), *Archie's TV Funnies* (1971–3), *Star Trek: The Animated Series* (1973–4), *He-Man and the Masters of The Universe* (1983–5), and *Ghostbusters* (1986–8). Most notably, Filmation was the very first animation company to adapt the iconic characters from the DC portfolio—starting with *The New Adventures of Superman* (1966–70), *The Adventures of Superboy* (1966–9), and *The Superman/Aquaman Hour of Adventure* (1967–8), followed by *The Adventures of Batman* (1968–70), *Shazam!* (1974–6), and the successive sequels to the Caped Crusader's adventures: *The Batman/Tarzan Adventure Hour* (1977–8), *Batman and the Super 7* (1980–1), and *The New Adventures of Batman* (1977–8).

Being an indirect offspring of the ABC's 1966 *Batman*, the Filmation material did share some similarities in terms of the general tone and narrative inputs, which could be recognized in the new animated guise. The voiceovers of the main duo Batman and Robin were provided respectively by Olan Soule and Casey Kasem, who clearly tried to imitate the original delivery of Adam West and Burt Ward from the live-action incarnation of both characters. Similarly, the new exploits drawn by Filmation's artists emulated the ridiculous stories of the predecessor, with a well-known rogues gallery including the Joker, Penguin, Riddler, and Mr. Freeze who all came up with elaborate stratagems. The very first episode—"My Crime is Your Crime"— showed the Joker and Penguin devising a diabolical scheme to make Batman wrongfully accuse them of crimes they have not committed and stand trial as a result. As modern fans openly admit, *The Adventures of Batman* and its Filmation follow-ups represented an artistic low-point for the character—given the technical shortcomings—while the goal was to exploit the fond memories of Adam West's show among the actual target audience (children) and to profit from the sentiment. The author of a throwback article published on the 13th Dimension website admits: "Let's face it: Filmation was schlock. Lovable schlock but schlock nonetheless. However, this was still a studio staffed with talented artists and you could really see it in the many evocative matte paintings and effects utilized throughout the show. I also really dig the vehicle designs."[7] There surely is not enough genuine innovation in the structures or themes of those stories to constitute any substantial reading of that particular rendition of the Bright Knight, but there may be another interesting element which manifested there, although not entirely intentionally, namely the previously intimated original appearance of the Dad Knight.

As Will Rodgers notes in his comprehensive study of the *Super Friends* animated show, Filmation's Batman may be considered the first implementation of Adam West's visually campy vigilante without the "double import" of the live-action show, which it delivered through double entendres or hidden meanings that may have gone over the heads of children but would have been grasped by adult viewers. Rodgers sums up the shlock-y original Batman cartoon thus: "The Batman series is reminiscent of the TV series, but without the camp" (2016: 35). If the original take on the campy Knight involved the clash of straight-faced characters and much more ludicrous settings with a surreptitious wink towards the adults, *The Adventures of Batman* focused on the straight heroes facing farcical perils but dispensed with the obscure allusions to the camp-related sexual aspect that was noticeable in the 1966 ABC production, as the inevitable effect of the artistic course that had been taken. However, *The Adventures of Batman*—a product developed with children in mind—intentionally focused on enhancing the cartoonish and "bizarre" elements, just as the Batman comics in the 1950s gave preference to science fiction to avoid any concerns about the heroes' sexuality as they explored fantastic worlds and faced even more unearthly dangers. Interestingly enough, when Filmation took over Batman's lore—continued later as part of Hanna-Barbera's cult line-up of various *Super Friends*, in a series launched in September 1973—the diegetic function of the character shifted tangibly from "partner" to a "parent" of Robin's, his young charge and associate in the crime-fighting business. Filmation's contribution—additionally augmented by Hanna-Barbera's tenure over the character in the 1970s, which followed the guidelines of the advocacy group Action For Children's Television—sanctioned an interpretation of the Dad Knight as a responsible and protective persona, always ready to give a moral lesson rather than a brutal punch. That particular portrayal was discussed by Will Rodgers who, in an analysis of the *Super Friends* series, aptly defined the "parenting" qualities of the core members of the supergroup: "Superman was a dad who could fly. Batman was a dad with a pointy-eared cowl and a utility belt. Aquaman was a dad who could swim. Wonder Woman was a mom with a lasso, bracelets, and an invisible jet, and Robin was a big brother sidekick" (2016: 41). Thus, the Dad Knight emerged out of the not-so-dark shadows of the Camp Knight, a figure possibly even more remote from the Dark Knight iteration of Batman and much more of a moral mentor than the Batusi-dancing Adam West, who now seemed a vigilante of adequately adult proportions in comparison. The combination of the visually aggressive Camp Batman and the overtly children-oriented Dad Knight would yield yet another crusader to close the list of the pre-Neon Knight embodiments, namely the Toy Knight or, as Jeffrey A. Brown recently phrased it, the mysterious (action) figure of the Cute Knight.

The story of the Cute Knight must be seen in relation to the 1966 Camp Knight, as the version of Batman portrayed by Adam West is an indisputable benchmark for many different Bright Knights over the years. With the advent of the future hit television show starring the Caped Crusader, another secondary offshoot appeared in 1966 when Ideal Toys launched a Batman variant of their original Captain Action doll, in the new 9-inch line of nine plastic superheroes (with Batman, Superman, Aquaman, Captain America, The Phantom, The Lone Ranger, Steve Canyon, Flash Gordon, and Sgt. Fury thrown into the mix as well). Obviously, due to the soaring popularity of the ABC production, the toy Batman was made to resemble the onscreen portrayal of the crusader, and imply that it was an official reproduction of Adam West's costumed look. However, in a study concerning the evolution of Captain Action, Michael Eury observes: "Ideal Toys did not include the blue bat-winged gloves that Batman wore in the comics and on television, despite their depiction on the package illustration. The box art also shows Batman wearing his traditional yellow utility belt, which is blue in the Captain Action version" (1999: 47). Although lacking direct correspondence with the depiction in audiovisual or graphic media, the desirability of that particular material form of Batman was boosted by other means—a wide range of extra gadgets and items that translated into extended playtime. As Eury recalls, besides the obvious cowl, uniform, or cape, the package included typical Caped Crusader's devices: the utility belt with a two-way radio, the baterangs (original spelling), a flashlight, a laser torch, grappling hook, and a bat rope with reel.

This original presentation of toy Batman follows the merchandise-driven logic of converting intellectual property into consumable objects, elucidated by Dan Fleming in his comprehensive study on the process of using film- or TV-based figures and sets to negotiate between the structure of the narrative to which a product refers and the user's spontaneous and individualized act of playing, whereby they conceive and add new meanings on top of the original media content. As Fleming observes, the process of redefining a children's toy, where it transitioned from miniaturized or simplified items of everyday use (e.g., trolleys, cars, or construction tools) to spectacle-based objects (imitating the characters and events that a child could witness in the cinema or watching television) sped up significantly after the advent of Saturday morning shows for kids in the 1980s, with *Transformers* and *G.I. Joe* franchises the most merchandise-oriented instances of such toyetic narratives. However, the process dates to much earlier times: in his analysis, Fleming looks as far back as 1811, citing the staging of *Mother Goose* in London, which gave rise to the local phenomenon of William West's "toy theatre." Essentially, it exploited a popular performance to garner children's interest in a line of items associated with the *Mother Goose* play available in West's department store. According to Fleming, such an approach to a toy—or an action or collectible figure in modern nomenclatural—which sees it as a component of multimedia spectacle produced a situation in which "With clearly established teams or characters and basic story structures that would generate endless plots around those characters, children could certainly watch and read plenty of given examples, but were also being encouraged to extend those with their own variations" (1996: 104). The subconscious danger of introducing characters like Batman into the sphere of officially undirected play modes generated by means of the growing legion of action figures and vehicles was probably the worst fear for any guardian of the Dark Knight's "true" canon—potentially culminating in loss of control over its dark nature due to the distinct logic of the toy manufacturers and increasing customization on the part of the consumers.

To see how that "customization" evolved in an historical and commercial context linked to some degree to Schumacher, one should probably consider one of the most notorious line of Batman-related toys: the 1994 series *Legends of Batman* produced by Kenner, a company associated with Batman merchandise for a long time. Although Kenner's approach to the plastic Caped Crusader—since the producer launched a massive Batman-centered offensive in 1990 with *The Dark Knight Collection*—always adhered to the logic of multiplying Batman's variations with changing accessories and/or color palettes of the toys (the 1992 range associated with *Batman Returns* included the lavishly yellow Deep Dive scuba-equipped Batman figure and the jungle-camo Air-Attack Batman), the *Legends of Batman* epitomized the most far-fetched vision of the plastic crusader. To name just a few products in the series, there were more "accurate" Batmen depictions, faithful to the contemporary comics and films, such as *Knightquest Batman* and *Knightsend Batman* (from the respective comic book sagas) and the *Crusader Batman*, the thoroughly unalloyed representation of the comic book Batman in the classic black and gray costume. Other items were definitely more troublesome for the Dark Knight's purists, as they included the *Viking Batman* with a giant ax, the *Cyborg Batman* with Terminator-like prosthetics, the *Samurai Batman* with an exaggerated Japanese katana, and the *Pirate Batman* crossing his sword with an equally pirate-esque villain Two-Face in an exclusive two-pack. The *Legends of Batman* toy line directly predated a later range of Batman-related products to accompany none other than the 1995 and 1997 Joel Schumacher Batman films, which would become the principal reference for the upcoming figures for mainstream consumers. Still, the approach adopted with the Schumacher-inspired toys had originated a little earlier in the history of the Toy Knight; its chief intention was to be able to develop and market Batman products that went beyond the limited, dark personification.

As previously noted, the most applicable term in the present-day discourse concerning Batman's manifestations as a toy or a consumer object was advanced by Jeffrey A. Brown in his analysis of the "cute" aesthetic, now commonly associated with literally every intellectual property that can be portrayed in such a guise. Brown asserts:

> In an effort to appeal to children (and nostalgic adults), superheroes have embraced the aesthetic of cuteness. Despite the contemporary Batman's dominant characterization as "grim and gritty," his likeness is everywhere as a friendly image for youngsters. With big eyes and an impish smile, Batman and so many other heroes exist as cuddly plush dolls, friendly Lego characters, silly cartoons and baby clothes. The "cuteness" of these variations reconfigures the violent and traumatic side of superheroes like Batman and repositions them as figures in need of our love and support … deserving of cuddles.
>
> (2018: 186–7)

With the powerful presence of the Dark Knight's likenesses by Funko Pop, Cosbaby, Lego, and Dorbz, the "privatization" of the erstwhile Batman character is apparently approaching its inevitable end seeing that, as Brown suggests, the very image of Batman and his material presence assumes a fragile and vulnerable aspect of a not-so-dark vigilante, positioning itself in a striking position to the "preferred" reading of a hypermasculine brute. This merchandise-driven journey from the early Captain Action-based iterations of Batman through the 1990s stylistically varied Kenner series towards the most recent festival of the Cute Knights heralds the ultimate and probably most outrageous reading of the Not-So-Dark Knight concept, which involves no less than the rejection of the "dark" characteristic of Batman as a deadly serious or utterly realistic hero. To draw again on Jeffrey A. Brown, the modern fascination with the Cute Knights may also be interpreted as willingness to acknowledge and rework the oft-noted element of toxic- or hypermasculine ideals that the figures of American superheroes celebrate, whereby the lonely vigilantes witness erosion of their established qualities of being invulnerable or tough in favor of being emotional and cute. According to Brown, "when superhero characters conform to an aesthetic of cuteness, they embody the exact opposite traits valorized in the original superhero style. Their cuteness exaggerates signs of softness, weakness and helplessness. In gender terms, the cute superhero is repositioned as feminized and infantilized—as sweet and cuddly rather than tough and strong" (2018: 197).

This final element of "cuteness" completes the triad of the Knights who appear to be the most remote from the popular image of the Dark Knight and the trinity of traits which, according to many, should never feature in an "accurate" depiction of Batman. The Camp Knight's intensity and humorous touch, the Dad Knight's nurturing approach, and the Cute Knight's emotional vulnerability and toyetic flavor no doubt combine to form a complex of the Bright Knight's most unsettling alternatives to the most classic Batman depictions, but do they really qualify to be treated as bad or wrong? The goal of this chapter was to underscore the principal concept of what is commonly referred to as the "floating signifier," although it is equally frequently confined to the numerous depictions of the Dark Knight that maintain the gray and black scheme. The thing is that there genuinely could and should be consent for the Rainbow Batmen to be in evidence in all narratives or consumer products, manifesting a wide range of Batman readings that could symbolically reposition the character outside his initial noir setting, in domains which do not have to satirize the figure but enable new thematic, artistic, and commercial exploits. Finally, it needs to be affirmed that there is a Batman for everyone, since the figure proved so flexible in accommodating even the most far-off forms and meanings, while each such incarnation should be considered viable and relatable due to changing historical or participatory contexts.

Nick Mamatas rightly concludes that, after all, Batman is nothing more than a set of musical and graphic images and connotations—a bat-shaped emblem and a bat-themed costume, a moody score by Danny Elfman and a catchy Neal Hefty song, topped with a depiction of the hero chasing the Joker that works well in dark hues and pastels alike (see Mamatas 2008: 47). The longevity of the character actually requires a more inclusive look at the tonal and thematic spectrum, which should involve as many disparate readings as possible to constantly diversify the Bat-universe populated already by the Dark Knights, Camp Knights, Dad Knights, Cute Knights, and many other Knights to come. Nevertheless, there is one particular vision among them which continues to be one of the most unique and the most unacceptable, irrespective of the many personal readings of what the Batman character may be, how he may be portrayed, and what new understandings he is capable of engendering. The variant in question is Joel Schumacher's Neon Knight: a cumulative sublimation of the main three earlier iterations of the Bright Knight discussed previously, substantially updated by virtue of Schumacher's very own style and Batman's overall transmedia presence in the 1990s. As a result, the singular vision of the Neon Knight would subsume the visual flair of the Camp Knight, the Dad Knight's emotional component, and the Cute Knight's merchandise-boosting strategy of supplying "customized" commercial Bat-items. On top of this combined triad of the main un-Darkened Knights, Joel Schumacher had his very own penchant for breaking and challenging the established artistic formulas, encompassing Batman's preconceived "seriousness."

Notes

1. Salazar Knight, "History of Batman: Batman's Real Nemesis: The Silver Age! / Silver Bat: Years 7-9," YouTube, 2018, https://www.youtube.com/watch?v=NdUczV04pwM&list=PLvOhZIQVv6hBvq8nIHmaVMfZP0ya5a0i7&index=83.
2. Geoff Boucher, "'Batman Inc.' gets busy as Grant Morrison Takes the Hero beyond 'blue-collar' Rage," Latimes.com, August 10, 2010, https://www.latimes.com/archives/blogs/hero-complex-blog/story/2010-08-10/batman-inc-gets-busy-as-grant-morrison-takes-the-hero-beyond-blue-collar-rage.
3. Patrick (H) Willems, "Learning to Appreciate Joel Schumacher's Batman," YouTube, 2020, https://www.youtube.com/watch?v=zKnGolObx0k&t=1333s&ab_channel=Patrick%28H%29Willems.
4. Andrew Goldman, "In Conversation: Joel Schumacher," Vulture.com, June 22, 2020, https://www.vulture.com/2020/06/joel-schumacher-in-conversation.html.
5. Anthony Borrelli, "Why Batman Movies' Obsession with Realism Hurts The Dark Knight," Screenrant.com, June 2, 2021, https://screenrant.com/batman-movies-realistic-grounded-problem-hurt-dark-knight/?fbclid=IwAR3T6zGMm9LmXsccm7Q00RR84z2b8nLcxAV3L2Hld1QT15dhdSVP1hn9YjA.
6. See Terence Towles Canote, "Batmania: How Batman Conquered America in 1966 Part Two," mercurie.blogspot.com, March 29, 2010, http://mercurie.blogspot.com/2010/03/batmania-how-batman-conquered-america_29.html.
7. Dan Greenfield, "13 Great Things about Filmation's 1968 Batman Cartoon," 13thdimension.com, May 20, 2021, https://13thdimension.com/13-great-things-about-filmations-1968-batman-cartoon/?fbclid=IwAR3NLrARCZVpWUxBsHbauLeRd5JLhNkacywmHjbj2E4PlJ0LhBxuLq1fH4c.

2

The Neon Knight unchained: Questionable choices and the ice-catching spectacle in *Batman Forever* and *Batman & Robin*

2.1 "Who's afraid of the big, black bat?": Joel Schumacher as a cinematic trespasser

Batman's exploits across a variety of media are often seen as a direct reflection of the specific times during which these productions were developed, catering to the respective social moods or conforming with the artistic preferences. This is the case with the *Batman* of 1966, which was heavily influenced by pop art and the original wartime silver screen portrayal of the Dark Knight—or rather Patriotic Knight for that matter—in the 1943 Columbia Pictures series *Batman*, with Lewis Wilson starring as the main character, essentially a masked government agent chasing the evil Japanese saboteur Dr. Daka. However, there are some iterations that happen to be out of or ahead of their time, waiting to be rediscovered or appreciated anew long after its initial release. This could be the case with Joel Schumacher's Batman duology of 1995 and 1997, as they saw conflicted receptions during their theatrical run and still seem to offend many Batman followers as the most convoluted attempts at a live-action feature starring Bob Kane's and Bill Finger's hero. Besides its lack of cosplay-generating energy—as demonstrated by Patrick H. Willems in the video commentary cited in the previous chapter—Schumacher's flicks still elicit discourse informed by the logic of "not like the others," which I discussed in the Introduction as an enduring strategy of reading Schumacher's films in the light of the earlier or later Batman blockbusters (marked by the distinctive visions given by Tim Burton and Christopher Nolan). Importantly, there is virtually no interest at all in understanding what the Schumacher-directed Batman movies are on their own and how they may stand out among their strong competition. To account for the usually unappreciated nature of Schumacher's Lighter Knight, one has to look at the broader legacy of the director's filmography, whose single yet most prominent motif is unapologetic courage to go against conventional tropes and expectations in any genre with which he had the opportunity to engage.

In the nineteenth episode of the animated show *The New Batman Adventures*—called "Legends of the Dark Knight," which is in the third season of the highly acclaimed *Batman: The Animated Series* and originally aired in the USA on October 10, 1998—an interesting cameo occurs as the episode itself tries to offer an anthology-like look at the perception of Batman. The main heroes here are Gotham City kids wandering through Gotham's streets and trying to figure out the "true" nature of the city's protector by suggesting their own ideas about the "definitive" representation of Batman which manifests here with a visual reference towards the aesthetical and conceptual models clearly inspired by the infamous 1960s Batman TV show (or the Sheldon Moldoff/Dick Sprang-driven run of the similarly family-friendly Batman comics from the same time period) and the much harsher and more brutal take obviously inspired by Frank Miller's *The Dark Knight Returns* from 1986. The structure of this particular animated episode is the clash between these two visions of Batman as a cheerfully colorful crusader on the one hand and a grim vigilante serving as a punishing force to all his enemies on the other. Quite symbolically, in the middle of the episode—after the 1960s-themed segment and just before the entrance of *The Dark Knight Returns*-influenced parable—a funny moment occurs as the main protagonists (referenced as Matt, Carrie, and Nick) are passing by a Gotham department store with a mannequin standing just before the main entrance of the shopping mall. Right there, a long-haired boy appears who seems to be deeply affected by the extravagant clothes hanging on the store's mannequin. He interrupts the protagonists' conversation about the "real" qualities of a Batman figure by adding his own take while at the same time hugging a pink scarf: "I love Batman. All those muscles, the tight rubber armor, and that flashy car. I heard he can drive off the walls." The only reaction he gets from his peers, however, is "Yeah, sure, Joel."

The genuine brilliance of this short nod to Joel Schumacher himself reflects the symptomatic split of the director's take on Batman, situating Schumacher's Knight rightfully but also tragically for his generally unfavorable perception by the majority of Batman fans somewhere between the post-Adam West sentiments and the Tim Burton/Frank Miller ideas about the seriousness of the main character, here manifested through the gothic lenses provided by Burton and the dystopian variant as portrayed in Miller's graphic novel. This brief scene from "The Legends of the Dark Knight" episode is also meaningful in its portrayal of the animated avatar "Joel" as some kind of wannabe window dresser, which serves accurately as a reference to Schumacher's real-life "artistic origins." Born on August 29, 1939 Joel Schumacher graduated from Parsons School of Design in 1965 and entered the film business originally as a production and costume designer with his debut in *Play It as It Lays*, directed by Frank Perry in 1972. As Schumacher himself often admitted, the real breakthrough in his film career came with Woody Allen's *Sleeper* in 1973, a wacky comedy referring to futuristic, dystopian themes, as Allen himself seemingly pushed the future director of *Batman Forever* into abandoning his designer position and moving into directing territory:

> It was Woody Allen who changed my life. In Christmas of 1971 he hired me to do the costumes on *Sleeper*. We happened to be in the Rocky Mountains, which was very unusual for Woody to leave New York, and he encouraged me to be a director, but said that first I had to write. He said "you're clever and funny, I think you can do it." And he gave some very good advice. He said the most important thing about writing is that you must finish it, and people must read it![1]

It seems that Schumacher actually took to heart Allen's comments, and Schumacher's philosophy of making films fundamentally entertaining for the audience became a common leitmotif in his filmography, which is filled with wacky ideas and over-the-top performances aimed primarily at the cinema of attractions' vibe that it should be firstly aesthetically pleasing. With this particular idea in mind, and at the beginning of Schumacher's retrospection which will come next, it is even more moving to look now at the widely commented-on apology from Schumacher for the final, controversial *Batman*

& Robin public reception. In 2009, Batman fans received special editions of the classic four Batman films, directed respectively by Burton and Schumacher, as part of *Batman: The Motion Picture Anthology 1989–1997*, formatted exclusively for the collector's DVD version. One of the main highlights of these newly re-edited discs was an impressive number of special features and bonus material documenting behind the scenes of the 1989–97 blockbusters. The main highlight of each film was a newly produced line of documentary features titled *Shadows of the Bat* with specific episodes called "Reinventing a Hero" (for *Batman Forever*) and "Batman Unbound" (for *Batman & Robin*), with the latter finishing with Schumacher's aforementioned humble and sincere statement: "If there's anybody watching this that, let's say, loved *Batman Forever* and went into *Batman & Robin* with great anticipation, if I disappointed them in any way then I really want to apologize. Because it wasn't my intention. My intention was just to entertain them."

The most euphemistic way to describe Joel Schumacher's movies would be to say that his filmography is full of "unconventional" features. Despite some generally praised productions, such as *The Lost Boys* (1987), *Falling Down* (1993), *A Time to Kill* (1996), *Tigerland* (2000), and *Phone Booth* (2002), it would be difficult to say that his movies were crowd-pleasers, since most provoked somewhat concerned reactions from the critics and audience alike. Aside from those few exceptions, it is difficult to name a Schumacher film that deserves to be called the director's high point—one that would represent the quintessential "Schumacher film," whatever this may actually mean. The very fact that there is no simple formula for Schumacher's "typical" work, and that the director himself is remembered by many mostly as "Batman's rubber nipples guy," should not lead to the misconception that his other work had nothing to offer filmgoers. On the contrary, Schumacher's filmography—spanning twenty-three feature-length films—presents quite a task when trying to single out a title one could define as "typical," "ordinary," or "conventional."

After Schumacher's death in 2020, in the rightly titled essay *Remembering Joel Schumacher: A Stylish Director Who Was Always Willing to Take Chances*, *Variety*'s Owen Gleiberman made interesting observations on the director's approach to filmmaking, pointing out Schumacher's unwillingness to be restricted by the established aesthetic premises or commercial expediency. Gleiberman notes:

> In each picture he directed, he tried for something, and it's to his credit that he never let too much caution—or good taste—rein him in. The best of his films were animated by a fluky humanity—an unruly sympathy for outsiders, and a desire to see where their odysseys would take him. Schumacher, at his best, was a rhythmic visual craftsman who knew how to stage a commercial film so that it imprinted itself on your mind's eye. Thirty years after seeing *Flatliners*, I can't shake its burnished look of macabre fluorescence, and 40 years after Schumacher's first film as a director, *The Incredible Shrinking Woman*, I still relish the contact high I got from the outlandish, gender-flipped spirit of its psychedelic design. ... Did he become a really good director? At his best, he did. That's because he never stopped taking the chances that make you one.[2]

Arguably, this notion of Schumacher as a wayward spokesman for the outsiders might be the best epitaph for a director whose portfolio included such varied yet commonly themed pieces as the 1990 odyssey of a spiraling American yuppie in the gruesome *Falling Down* or a disfigured opera singer becoming a haunting stalker in the bombastic and over-produced *The Phantom of the Opera* (2004), the venture of a group of modern Frankenstein-like medics outside the liminal space of life and death in *Flatliners* (1990) and a similar journey of young soldiers to the eponymous no man's Tigerland, which exists between the land of their previous carefree life and the anticipated horrors of war. The first thing one notices about Schumacher's works is that sympathy for the lawbreakers and lawbreaking as a mode of living and creating—since, as Gleiberman stated, taking chances was probably the underlying strategy in most of his films—result in their discordant reception. Without being too Freudian about that particular trait of Joel Schumacher as a filmmaker, there may be a significant clue in the rebellious attitude dating back to a young age which—as Schumacher himself admitted—had a substantial influence on both his moral and artistic preferences. In a very honest and outspoken interview with *Vulture* journalist Andrew Goldman, Schumacher was asked explicitly how his experiences growing up in 1950s New York City had impacted his homosexual and drug-related coming-of-age at the time:

> The whole thing started as a joke, when I was asked by journalists some question and I said, "I'm overpaid, I'm overprivileged, and I'm oversexed." That was a joke. Most gay men have many partners because it's not a very "no" culture. I started drinking at 9, smoking at 10, and fooling around sexually when I was 11. ... I don't know if it was legal or illegal, I just knew you didn't talk about it. But I had three girlfriends I had sex with, and some of the guys on my baseball team, a couple guys in high school. I had my first love affair when I was 15 to 17, and he was 17 to 19. That was the first time I remembered really being in love with someone, or let's say, infatuated. But we both had girlfriends. ... At that particular time, there were no magazines that dealt with homosexuality, no newspaper articles, there weren't books, there was no education about all of this. I just was who I was.[3]

The most significant insight from that particular conversation is Schumacher's very accepting, unbiased, even quite idealistic attitude, evident in the disclosure about private sexual openness. It may explain why later Schumacher gave preference to a variety of characters equally openly interested in overstepping the boundaries or going beyond the acceptable in their cinematic exploits. This non-schematic and non-labeling artistic strategy was actually noted by the director himself in a conversation with Matthew Hays of *Advocate*. The latter recalled: "I bluntly asked Schumacher why he avoided being called gay. 'I'm a big opponent of labels,' he shot back without pause. 'African-American judge, Jewish vice-presidential candidate, lesbian congresswoman, transgendered military officer, whatever. I don't recall anyone referring to Bill Clinton as our Caucasian, heterosexual, WASP, male ex-president. In other words, he's normal and everyone with a label isn't.'"[4] This perfectly tallies with the aforementioned difficulty in defining Schumacher's films and themes in terms of the strict conventions of standard filmmaking. Both visually and tonally, it would be reasonable to assert that Schumacher was not actually interested in conforming to any paradigms or style in his films, and a less discerning viewer would see them as a traditional horror/vampire tale (*The Lost Boys*), a war drama (*Tigerland*), a journalist's biopic (*Veronica Guerin*, 2003), a David Fincher's *Seven* rip-off (*Phone*

Booth), a medical thriller (*Flatliners*), and a neo-noir detective story (*8mm*, 1999). However, what might define the "Schumacher style" of directing is the unexpected or even largely unwelcome twist with which Schumacher invested almost all of his creations, subverting expectations when that unpredictable ingredient was added to the final onscreen mix. Far from being a genre-specific cinematic purist, Joel Schumacher espoused a different artistic agenda which made him a radical cinematic rule breaker, one who took a pleasure in going against whatever others might have anticipated, for the sake of the heroes and characters that likewise transgressed against the narrative and stock characteristics.

The impact of the autobiographical element on Schumacher's work was also recognized by Tegan O'Neil, whose analysis of the various incarnations of Batman included Joel Schumacher's take on the character. In O'Neil's opinion, "it would be very difficult to argue Schumacher would have been unaware, on any level, of what he was doing when he made *Batman & Robin*. He knew camp. He knew arch. He knew gay history, both comic and tragic. He certainly understood queer subtext."[5] A queer reading of Schumacher's films may offer yet another relevant perspective in which the transgressive aspect of his features actually works, consciously challenging the attitudes towards his narratives through their shared striving to subvert the norm with visual or tonal extremity. Considering the typically "masculine" genres with which Schumacher was working—a vampire story, a war story, or a superhero story in the case of Batman—the queer trope reveals an interesting aspect: a deliberate attempt at undermining heteronormativity, whether it was the sexual characteristics of the protagonist or the overall status of a particular genre, which may possess its own "sexuality," reflected in the generally presumed nature of the story's resolution or in the gender roles assigned to individual characters. As such, it is not difficult to conceive that Schumacher's films overtly "queered" Hollywood patterns from the inside, since much of his work were tales that undercut heteronormativity and sought to challenge the "norm" outlined at the beginning of each feature. A typical structure of a Schumacher tale would start with the acceptable or even palpably dull mundanity or predefined model which, as the film unfolded, pushed the initial normality further and further into the extreme.

Schumacher's debut as a feature-length movie director—with the 1981 *The Incredibly Shrinking Woman*—was the forerunner of this approach, portraying its main protagonist played by Lily Tomlin as a "typical" 1980s housewife, whose figure and surroundings reflect the most stereotypical notions of suburban culture and gender-specific roles. Considering the involvement of both directors in the Batman franchise, it is curious to see how close *The Incredibly Shrinking Woman* actually is to Tim Burton's *Edward Scissorhands* (1991), being a similar suburbia-set comedy horror which, as with the latter, confronts the American archetype with fantasy. Significantly, however, the perspectives of both creators are quite distinct—in Burton's gothic fairy tale it is the protagonist who comes from the abnormal realm, whereas in the Schumacher story the inconspicuous Pat Kramer becomes the heroine, and whose exposure to chemicals reveals to her a new facet of the household, an aberration in a normal setting. The obstacles that the shrinking Pat Kramer has to deal with multiply in the course of the film, with more and more absurd and extreme consequences of the shrinking process; the ultimate complication involving an secret, evil organization, who plot to cause humankind's shrinking crisis. Schumacher's debut is actually a fairly open criticism of worldwide corporations as the scheme of the film's antagonists is well summarized by Pat Kramer herself when she says that the cabal controlling global material addiction needs to make the everyday consumers smaller to feel bigger again. Still, the film itself definitely offers a preliminary statement that would resonate in later Schumacher's endeavors, since it engages in this "trespassive" process, quite literally mixing suburban drama with ridiculous science fiction and spy thriller, and adding a substantial secondary character in the finale, in which a highly intelligent gorilla becomes Kramer's last ally. All this yields a genre-unspecific feature which starts with a pastel setting and concludes with the heroine discovering her new "growing" abilities. Also, *The Incredibly Shrinking Woman* somewhat surreptitiously pursues a queering narrative, with the ostensibly unheroic housewife in the very center of a sci-fi/thriller-like story, and evident de-masculinization of Pat Kramer's poor husband, whose portrayal is dominated by two main characteristics: he is a passive and obedient inferior employee in a company that wants to profit from Pat's current state, as well as a disappointed and resentful lover compelled to sexual abstinence caused by his wife's shrinking.

The Incredibly Shrinking Woman may be interpreted as an initial exercise for Schumacher's subsequent transgressive experiments. Its echoes reverberate throughout the director's filmography, as the invariable trope of his work is clashing the norm with the extreme in a deliberately amplified visual package. Schumacher's opus magnum in the opinion of most cinemagoers—*Falling Down*—is also somewhat a trespassive story, as the journey of the main character, Bill, played by Michael Douglas, begins in the most "typical" American setting, i.e., in a vehicle traffic jam, only to continue on an invariably deviant route through America's landscape to reach the house of his ex-wife for his daughter's birthday. Once again, Schumacher serves his own twist in Bill's tale—on the one hand he is a determined father, ready to stand up to vicious city gangs and a maniacal neo-fascist in his own lair, while at the same time his original social status declines as he loses his existing family connections, has to move in with his mother, and gets fired from his job. *Falling Down* is replete with meaningful scenes reflecting the upside-down version of a real-life myoma and yuppie in one, who violates the social spaces where this "kind" of American man's failure is unwelcome, building increasingly acute contrasts between Bill and places or circumstances on his way. In one of the most in-your-face sequences, Bill trespasses on an exclusive golf club and, after a brief quarrel with its wealthy members, he shoots a golf cart causing one of them to have a heart attack. Ultimately, however, Bill is yet another pitiable, unmanly hero rather than an actual menace, as Schumacher deals the unfortunate soul the final blow in the closing duel with a police officer. The about-to-retire detective, played by Robert Duvall, shoots Bill without knowing that the latter is armed with no more than a toy pistol in his pocket.

Schumacher's interest in trespassing—understood as both actual venture into unprecedented spaces and/or dealing with a rejected or obscure moral and aesthetic domain—is apparent in virtually all his works, including the more escapist narratives such as *The Lost Boys*, in which a gang of rock n roll vampires invade a small conservative community to culminate in a *Goonies*-like finale, with juvenile vampire-hunters brutally disposing of the bloodsuckers as red splatters profusely throughout. In his more subtle pieces, e.g., *Flatliners*, *8mm*, *Veronica Guerin*, and *Phone Booth*, the audience is once again confronted with boundary-crossing tales, including medical students' experiments with NDEs to divine the nature of human passing, the journey of a private detective and a devoted husband and father into the world of hardcore pornography, a young journalist's crusade to explore Ireland's drug underworld, and a rephrased concept from the cult *Seven* by David Fincher, in which a social vigilante traps a publicist in a phone booth call and unravels his private life by forcing him to confess his sins for all to hear. In a curious coincidence, the last cinema feature directed by Schumacher starring Nicole Kidman and Nicolas Cage as rich owners of a luxury mansion attacked by a group of thieves is titled *Trespass* (2011), as if Schumacher himself wished to convey the core meaning of his films, in which the aesthetic assumptions of the audience and the foundations of fictional existence of the protagonists were both taken hostage.

Looking for the "definitive" emanation of Schumacher's artistic transgression, one would have to consider his Batmen or the one other work which qualifies as evident and generally acclaimed act of "Schumacherism" in film, i.e., the 2000 *Tigerland*. For many reasons, that peculiar take on the Vietnam War is a trademark in his cinematic storytelling, bringing together all the vital themes and character types that Schumacher was clearly fond of. First of all, the eponymous "hero" of the story—the so-called Tigerland territory—is a liminal space in itself, the last site between homeland bases and the unknown ground of the Vietnam conflict. Tigerland is supposed to offer real-life combat experience, with the recruits having to face the actual conditions of brutal and nonsensical warfare; a curious simulation, and simultaneously another area where a direct act of trespassing takes place, as the soldier novices are the intruders who enter savage wilderness to fight an undefined foe. Schumacher's take on the American forces in the context of the Vietnam War derives from the director's perennial interest in exploring the act of violating predefined areas, whereby a group of heroes face utterly new circumstances, outside their previous experiences or expectations. To this end, Schumacher conceives one of his most iconic and fully developed protagonists, Bozz played by Collin Farrell. Bozz is yet another recruit sent to complete training before participating in the ongoing war, but he is clearly depicted as the ill-fitting element in a homogenous group of determined young men. Bozz is a rebellious free spirit who openly disrespects his superiors and introduces an element of chaos and doubt into the factory-like formation of cannon fodder. The principal conflict between Bozz and the group's most gung-ho recruit Wilson (played by Shea Whigham) follows Schumacher's typical opposition, where an absurd individual like Wilson, bloodthirsty and incensed at Bozz's frivolity, is set against Farrell's character, who actively seeks to undermine the hypermasculine nature of the entire setting, though not to escape from it (as throughout the story Bozz develops a unique rapport with the other soldiers) but rather to subconsciously deconstruct the image of a soulless soldier. Sustaining the essential motif, Bozz is precisely a trespassing type of hero, who encroaches on the space of Vietnam-related, testosterone-driven imagery and ushers in an unexpected element of likability and common sense into this mechanical mode of producing a regular army.

An interesting insight into *Tigerland*'s chief premise is provided by Schumacher himself who, in a 2000 interview with Charlie Rose, shared some significant remarks about that particular picture. Asked to highlight the main points in his story of the Vietnam War Schumacher commented:

> It's really not about the Vietnam. It looms like Darth Vader somewhere out there ... I wanted the audience what it would be like to be a teenager ... yanked by the draft ... out of a basic Judeo-Christian society where their church, their synagogue, their school, their parents, their life has been. 'Be a gentleman, don't be violent, be a nice guy ...' ... yanked out of that. Now become an unquestioning mass murderer in eight weeks .... It's about a reluctant hero ... what you see in this young man ... is he has no desire to do the right thing or be a hero and he does it angrily despite himself.[6]

Later on during this conversation, Schumacher readily sees a figure reminiscent of himself in Collin Farrell's Bozz—a stubborn individual who does not take anything for granted and has the courage to talk back or disobey the authorities if he feels it is right. Although it is always risky to read a single text as a direct manifestation of the author's own attitudes or preferences, it seems that *Tigerland* is a Joel Schumacher film through and through—from exploring the geographically liminal space between American and Vietnamese territory to Bozz's mindset, which compels him to question the conflict itself as well as the presumed norms that the largely acquiescent teenagers are expected to comply with. One could use this particular approach to explain Joel Schumacher's general treatment of the "expected norms" of filmmaking, as he often emulates Bozz's recalcitrance and unwillingness to follow the established patterns. However, this may sound quite strange when speaking about a director who had earned a reputation for bringing in substantial revenue from his John Grisham's adaptations or, most notably, taking the helm of the Batman franchise. The trick is to notice that rebellious nature even in Schumacher's most blatantly commercial productions, which nevertheless delivered rather unexpected visions which went against the predefined aesthetic norms, just like Bozz's actions exposed the army's toxic and unproductive schemes.

In a brief outline of the most essential of Joel Schumacher's contributions to the Batman cinematic series of the 1990s, Akiva Goldsman mentioned one particular thing: "The movie (*Batman Forever*) was bigger and more ... welcoming."[7] This one simple statement epitomizes all the crucial changes that are relevant today with regards to the director's impact on the Dark Knight's exploits. Without doubt, his approach was way more bombastic in terms of visual design, but it is the other quality asserted by Goldsman—the "welcoming" aspect—that requires an explanation here. On the face of it, Goldsman must be thinking about the 1995 *Batman Forever*, a more family-friendly and broadly acceptable crowd-pleaser than the dark and twisted gothic fairy tale of Tim Burton's previous *Batman Returns* (1992). As I explain later, Joel Schumacher was brought in as Batman's director in an effort to reclaim a more inclusive iteration of the character, one more appropriate for regular moviegoers and commercial licensees alike. However, hiring Schumacher proved to have a much greater impact on Batman's aesthetic and tonal make-up, as the author succeeded in retelling Batman mythology relying on his very own taste, trespassing the norms of a guaranteed blockbuster for the sake of an unsettlingly more nuanced subtext grafted into the character's lore and meaning. The "welcoming" aspect should rather be construed as a direct corollary of Schumacher's original need for un-labeling since his version of Batman is just that—a dissonant addition to a strictly delineated territory that the director now expands with unprecedented motifs and the most aggressively colorful embodiment to supplant the previous noir-driven homage from Burton.

Evidently, Joel Schumacher changed the look and the feel of Batman onscreen and yet remained true to his personal inclination of provoking and subverting the general notion of the character. The visual nature of *Batman Forever* and *Batman & Robin* demonstrate it abundantly, as Schumacher took the "graphicness" of the heroic exploits into the most absurd and most visually extreme territories that Batman had ever seen. A *New York Times* reviewer observed: "He steered 'the Batman franchise into its most baroque territory' .... But it may be the most succinct encapsulation of the Schumacher style: a big and gaudy, colorful and stylish, cheerfully unapologetic crowd-pleaser."[8] For his part, Schumacher would probably not mind calling himself a skillful craftsman rather than a sophisticated artist. Charlie Rose recalls Schumacher say in one of their many conversations: "You said at one point that you know it is very hard to believe you have a calling and then realize you're not gifted,"[9] which quite sufficiently attests to Schumacher's honesty in seeing himself, as he put it, as a provider of the artistic equivalent of fast food: "There's a menu out there. The great thing about film is that there are Big Macs, there are little Polish restaurants, there's Thai food and you know and they don't all have to be compared to one another. Sometimes a great Big Mac is just wonderful and I think that we lose sight of that sometimes."[10] Probably, the most unexpected thing about this Big Mac-filmmaking is that despite Schumacher's own seemingly modest intentions his fast-food menu did feature a unique dish of his disconcerting and offbeat view of the world around him, of which his Batman films are the most notorious.

Considering that in his pursuit to un-darken the Dark Knight the director sought to please the audience, one may paraphrase the iconic final statement made by Matthew McConaughey's character in the second successful adaptation of Grisham's court drama in Schumacher's *A Time To Kill* (1996). In the movie, defense attorney Jack Brigance (McConaughey) delivers his closing argument, calling for empathy towards a vigilante-turned father Carl Lee Hailey (played by Samuel L. Jackson) who had stood trial for killing his daughter's murderers. Brigance is trying to sway the largely white jury to acknowledge the tragedy of an African-American girl brutally violated by local hillbillies. Anyone asking for Schumacher's Batman to be recognized could rehash Brigance's brilliant speech: "Can you see him? His ridiculed, ignored, rejected, soaked in neon vision—left to oblivion. Can you see him? I want you to picture that particular Batman. Now imagine he is the Batman that you cherish." Since the overall hallmarks of a Schumacher film have been established, now is the opportunity to answer the question cited in the title of this section, yet another quote from a Schumacher character—the villainous Jim Carrey's The Riddler in *Batman Forever*: "Riddle me this, riddle me that. Who's afraid of the big, black bat?" As "fear" may not be the best way to put it, it is most certainly Joel Schumacher who encourages us to trespass on uncharted Batman territory and solicit some recognition for the unorthodox, tradition-defying vision of this iconic hero outside his most widespread depiction based on visual and psychological darkness. And so, finally, enter the Neon Knight.

2.2 Tim Burton's Noir-tmare before Christmas vs. Joel Schumacher's camp noir: Embracing a living comic book as a visual thriller

If there is one specific scene that has "Joel Schumacher's Batman" written in screaming capitals all over it and reveals him as an intruder—given the previous iterations of Batman in the Hollywood blockbuster formula—it has to be the final shot of *Batman Forever*, repeated later in the ending of *Batman & Robin* also—which shows both main protagonists (with Batgirl joining the set in 1997) running towards the camera against the background of the sharply illuminated Bat-signal, to the accompaniment of Elliot Goldenthal's upbeat march. That single shot alone could be used as an eloquent representation of Schumacher's fundamental aesthetic choice for his Batman: a hybrid "camp noir" style, as contrasted with what Tim Burton had opted for. The latter's more reasonable and artistically acceptable fusion of noir elements and expressionistic imagery had already been in evidence in the classic German Expressionist cinema of the 1920s and 1930s, in its American variety of equally classic Universal Studios' horrors, and in the monster fests from the British Hammer Studios in which Burton himself was so invested. Before discussing Schumacher's camp noir aesthetic which lent his Knight the final neon look, one cannot fail to consider Burton's last Batman work—the 1992 sequel to his commercial juggernaut of 1989—which nevertheless had met with a peculiar reception, as the concerned public found it too much of a "Burton film" rather than a "Batman film."

As inevitable as the idea of a sequel to the 1989 *Batman* was to everybody after the movie's phenomenal theatrical run with approximately $412 million in worldwide revenue, it so happened that the most crucial person in the entire project—director Tim Burton himself—was not particularly convinced that a follow-up to the character's arc was necessary. As numerous sources have reported over the years, the production of *Batman* was so stressful and so consuming for the young creator that for a time he simply did not see any point in carrying on with the job; of all involved, Burton himself was probably the most unhappy with how the first film finally turned out. As Mark S. Reinhart recalls, the bosses at the Warner Bros. Studios were so determined to sign Burton on again—as he had now become a fully-fledged author following public acclaim for *Batman*'s original noirish style—that they decided to lure the director by giving him free rein to do things his way that time. According to Reinhart, "Warner Bros. was able to heighten Burton's interest in directing the *Batman* sequel by giving him far more creative control over the film that he was allowed to have over *Batman* – for the *Batman* sequel, he would be both producer and director" (2013: 124). In time, however, the profound confidence the studio had in making *Batman 2* as a Tim Burton movie in every respect eventually proved its handicap, just as "Burtonism" had been considered the greatest advantage of the 1989 release and the reason for its appreciation. With regard to the divisive reception of the second installment, Glen Weldon rightly observes, "*Batman Returns* was destined to become what it ultimately turned out to be: *un film de* Tim Burton ... with Batman in it" (2016: 174).

As the story of the two Batmen by Tim Burton has already been recounted in detail in many insightful monographs over the years, this section will focus mainly on the qualities of Burton's second take on the character as well as consider its financial and artistic impact, which resulted in bringing in Joel Schumacher as a replacement for Burton in June 1993. Concerning the prospective sequel, Burton was interested in the opportunity offered by Warner Bros. Studios, whereby they wanted to do things differently this time and strictly follow the director's wishes, unlike with the first film when Burton was just a young creator thrown into a tangle of visions of the producers, merchandisers, as well as other members of film's creative team. Significantly enough, Burton made a profound statement in the introduction to the official *Batman Returns Official Movie Book* edited by Michael Singer:

> So let me begin by just saying that *Batman Returns* is not really a sequel to *Batman*. It doesn't pick up where the first film left off. The sets for Gotham City are completely new. There are lots of new elements in the visuals and storyline that haven't been seen before. Even Batman's costume has been revised. The point was to make it all feel fresh and new. It was the only way I could envision the movie.
>
> (1992: 6)

It would not be unreasonable to see the 1989 *Batman* and the 1992 *Batman Returns* as separate projects, although they do share common yet occasionally very sketchy cinematic continuity and general tone of story. However, the substantial changes introduced by the sequel suffice to set it apart from the previous installment. As the aforementioned Glen Weldon noted, *Batman Returns* is a strictly authorial project with all the necessary ingredients of cinematic "Burtonism," with the main character adjusted to dovetail with that artistic and thematic environment rather than the other way around.

Ironically, this was the primary reason behind the earlier success; after all, the Batman persona as defined by Burton fitted perfectly into the gallery of Burtonesque characters such as Edward Scissorhands, Jack Skellington, Ed Wood, and Willy Wonka: misunderstood, eccentric, introverted, and socially awkward geniuses that echoed Burton's own interest in all kind of misfits whom the world considered monsters. The amplified "Burtonism" in *Batman Returns* resulted in a much more confusing final outcome, since the film happened to be far keener on showcasing monstrous wretches—notably Danny de Vito's hideous Penguin and Michelle Pfeiffer's alluring Catwoman—than a traditional superhero flick, while its interest in the main protagonist was also very limited. Weldon concludes: "*Batman Returns* ... exudes every stylized, quintessentially Burtonesque artisanal quirk in the toolbox—except the sense of melancholy. Without it, the film powers through the confusing switchbacks of its plot, cynically risking nothing, and about nothing except itself" (2016: 178).

As the quintessential Tim Burton film with Batman in it, *Batman Returns* is in some ways more an artistic and spiritual derivative of Burton's later animated *The Nightmare Before Christmas* (1993) than a descendant of the original *Batman* from 1989. Its final form and atmosphere could be encapsulated as a "Noir-tmare before Christmas" story that tries to combine the previous *Batman*'s noir roots with a much more gruesome aspect and a tinge of Christmas mood, so meaningful for many films by Burton. As a result, the 1992 feature certainly disappointed some of the expectations aroused by the 1989 blockbuster, namely that it would deliver a much more personal or even strictly artistic touch than the full-blown spectacle of three years prior. Still, there are several elements of note here that directly anticipate Joel Schumacher's reinterpretation of the franchise in 1995. The first is the depiction of the main superhero who, as previously observed, was clearly conceived as yet another entry in the gallery of Burton's rejects. For many years, one of the fundamental issues the fans and critics had with *Batman Returns* was evident lack of interest in the Noir-tmare Knight on Burton's part. The director himself admitted on multiple occasions that this was precisely how—in his opinion—a Batman-focused story should be told.

The series of Tim Burton interviews edited by Kristian Fraga includes a conversation between the director and Marc Shapiro concerning that reluctant portrayal of the comic book good-doer, in which the following is disclosed: "We chose not to try and uncover any more skeletons about this guy. Batman has always been a tricky character because, by his nature, he wants to remain in the shadows. He's a tough character because he's so internalized" (Fraga 2005: 91). It may seem to be a direct response to the general concerns regarding Batman's characteristics—i.e., those of an emotionally inaccessible avenger—but it is particularly interesting that the fans criticized *Batman Returns* for being more of a "Burton-Man Returns" narrative. This is profoundly and quite symbolically evinced in Mark S. Reinhart's Batman filmography, where the author openly expresses his own disappointment as a fan with the exceedingly personal depiction of his favorite character:

> From this Batman's fan perspective, Tim Burton must be held accountable for most all of *Batman Returns* failings. In the film, he chose to depict Batman,

Penguin, and Catwoman in ways that made them almost unrecognizable so that they reflect his own morose sensibilities—they are not so much *Batman* characters in the film as they are "Burton" characters. Simply put, *Batman Returns* isn't about Batman, it is about Burton's perception of modern urban life as a lonely, hopeless existence. If Burton wanted to make a film with this particular message, he should have made it using characters of his own invention.

(2013: 137)

Burton's far-reaching retelling in his second endeavor with Batman's lore engendered somewhat unexpected responses from the studio and the audience, who experienced *Batman Returns* in the regular setting of blockbuster entertainment as a subversive act of being shown an "art-oriented" rather than franchise-oriented film: "critics seem to be amused by the idea that people were going to see *Batman Returns* hoping for an action-packed good time, and would instead be walloped over the head by Burton's morose, edgy 'art film'" (Reinhart 2013: 132). Indeed, the 1992 motion picture had been designed as a virtually anti-franchise production, both thematically and commercially, seeing that,

> While the commonly accepted arc for Batman movies sees him leaving the shadows and learning the basic benefits of teamwork, *Returns* seems like a step back from the traditions of his story's progression. ... Burton and his collaborators obviously don't much believe in the efficacy of Batman's heroism—a step away from the majestic end of the first film, which has Batman being tacitly deputized via the shining glow of the Bat-Signal. The Batman of *Returns* always seems to be working through something. His escapades don't feel like derring-do attempts to rid the city of the evil that stole his parents, nor do they ever unfold in that direction, like we see in *The Batman*—they're more like pressure-valve releases for a disturbed individual.[11]

It was apparently the anti-franchise formula used by Burton that had the most impact on the decision to have the director replaced. Once again, the accompanying debate about the backlash from American parents concerned about the grotesque mood of *Batman Returns* became almost a meme in today's terms, with a number of televised reports from 1992 widely available now through streaming services. Ironically enough, the artistic mandate that Warner Bros. gave Burton at the beginning of production brought about the inevitable consequence of such a strategy: a highly unconventional attempt to deliver a challenging movie as opposed to a bland gadget generator. In a documentary about the origins of *Batman Returns*, Sam Hamm—the co-author of the 1989 *Batman* screenplay—commented: "The movie itself was never presented as you know as a child-friendly movie,"[12] and the film's chief screenwriter Daniel Waters admitted likewise: "I've seen the movie with audiences much more than Tim has. I actually go to a lot of theatres and it was always great—the lights coming up after *Batman Returns* and it was like kids crying and people acting like they were punched in the stomach, like they've been mugged. The part of me was … like 'oops.'"[13]

Batman Returns is an intriguing case of what is clearly an anti-franchise approach clashing with a franchise-focused perception. The film did manage to market a vast range of Batman-related memorabilia, but it was the overall response from the parents of young viewers that eventually prompted hysteria around the release. In one of the most memorable US television reports on the unwelcome showing of *Batman Returns*, namely *A Closer Look: Batman Returns' Impact on Children* from July 1992, one of guests—a child critic (he was ten years old at the time) Danny Slaski—stated that "[i]t was a total attack against kids, the whole movie. Everything that kids love was being used against them." The same sentiment was expressed sometime later by a guest on the show, allegedly a concerned mother of a young girl:

> I do think that the marketing confused us a little and a lot of the reason that we went to see it was based on what my memories of Batman were from when I was a child .... The whole series of comic books that were very, very defined—good versus evil. It was not a real violence, rather inferred violence and it was justice and morality.[14]

The common denominator here is the fundamental allegation that Burton failed to respect the conventional expectations of Batman's appearance, which— as Slaski argued—was anything but child-friendly entertainment. Curiously enough, the 1989 iteration of Batman could have hardly been defined as a movie appropriate for children, with its explicit depictions of Jack Nicholson's Joker's violent acts, though the main reason behind the more widespread approval may have been that the heroes and villains in the 1989 *Batman* were fairly unambiguous, and the aforementioned opposition of good versus evil was clear. In the more Burton-centric *Batman Returns* the structure of this classical conflict is rendered more complex—with the lackluster figure of Batman, the center of gravity shifts towards the outrageously aggressive performances of De Vito and Pfeiffer epitomizing Burton's tortured souls, the misfits who, having been rejected by the society, adopt more brutal modes of action. Catwoman's main narrative premise is taking revenge on her former boss while Penguin's biblical plan to kill all Gotham City's firstborns is a call for twisted justice rooted in his own Moses-like fate. Undoubtedly, both villains are figures of the Burtonesque persuasion, given their ambiguous motives and disputable behavior, rather than comic book faithful interpretations of a cat-burglar and a greedy, bird-themed thief. That must have been a major factor compounding the confusion of probably the most crucial audience of the Batman sequel—namely the licensees.

Tim Burton himself recalls in a somewhat funny vein: "I think I upset McDonald's. (They asked) 'What's that black stuff coming out of the Penguin's mouth. We can't sell Happy Meals with that!'"[15] The involvement of merchandise-focused enterprises such as McDonald's or Kenner at an early stage in the *Batman Returns* production was also reflected in the extensive material and publications concerning the film, which referred to Burton's general loathing of filmmaking that prioritized merchandise. The absurdity of such an approach was even more obvious considering that—as noted previously—the entire film crew were well aware at the outset that this particular production would be more director- than commercially driven. The striking contrast between the colorful action figures and Happy Meal toys on the one hand and the gritty tone and unsettling imagery on the other was highlighted by Mark S. Reinhart, who stated that "[a]ll of their efforts to market the film would be a construed as a cynical effort to entice young children to see a movie that they really had no business seeing" (2013: 129). Paradoxically, what was unintentionally a family film intentionally relied on Burton's taste and artistic preferences. If

1989 gave the world a Batman made by Tim Burton, the year 1992 offered it a Burton-Man based on Batman iconography. Consequently, neither the fans, the executives, the critics, nor the family audience were satisfied. Still, with Burton's contribution made extreme, yet another denizen of Batman's artistic multiverse emerges—a Noir-tmare Knight born out of the fascinating combination of Burton's Christmas horror, the noir leftovers from his previous work, and a trio of the sinister yet internally tragic characters. At present, acclaim for the film is growing among the fans, but it was clear at the time that a correction course was needed. The goal was to extricate the Dark Knight from his Noir-tmare embodiment, revive public interest in the franchise, and regain the trust of Batman's most essential audience: the licensees. The task was entrusted to Joel Schumacher but, even though he managed to breathe life into the franchise which yielded renewed box-office and merchandise revenue, Warner Bros. Studios once again got something they had probably wanted to avoid: another excessively individual vision which alienated many of the conservative Batman consumers.

Recently, Michael Keaton—the onscreen Batman in the two Tim Burton's movies— reminisced on his meeting with Joel Schumacher: "I remember one of the things that I walked away going, 'Oh boy, I can't do this' …. He asked me, 'I don't understand why everything has to be so dark and everything so sad,' and I went, 'Wait a minute, do you know how this guy got to be Batman? Have you read … I mean, it's pretty simple.'" [16] Right there, at the very outset, the most significant attribute of Schumacher's vision of Batman becomes clear— the un-darkening process so unimaginable for the majority of Batman fans. And yet, is it such a travesty to even envisage that kind of Batman's appearance? As already stated, Schumacher's idea for Batman—embodied in the Neon Knight—was based on three distinct yet complementary predecessors who had already radically redefined the Dark Knight into much brighter iterations of the character. What if the apparently novel variant created by Schumacher is just another form of hybridization, as the director succeeded in merging the Camp Knight, the Dad Knight, and the Cute Knight, blended in a soupcon of the Noir-tmare Knight from Burton's duology, to ultimately arrive at the camp noir style as seen in *Batman Forever* and *Batman & Robin*. To appreciate the nuances of the Neon Knight as he turned out, the first thing is to comprehend

Schumacher's visual conception for Batman, which attempted to combine highly cartoony and campy influences with the post-Burtonesque neo-gothic and neo-noir imagery.

Commonly in Batman's legacy, the two duologies of "Burtonverse" and "Schumacherverse" are often approached as complementary to each other in narrative and aesthetic terms, though Schumacher is treated as a tonally disturbing supplement to the previously established post-expressionistic agenda of Tim Burton's. According to Ben Aldis,

> The most glaring difference would be the visuals. Gotham City seemingly regenerated overnight, becoming a garish and cartoony town with no sign of the original quasi-40s noir world. Dialogue and characters are also light-hearted and overblown; villains like Arnold Schwarzenegger's Mr. Freeze or Jim Carrey's The Riddler acted more silly than sinister, and boasted nonsensical schemes of world-domination. Humor was less organic and more campy and on-the-nose, which unfortunately undercut attempts at drama (i.e. Alfred lying on his death bed). Perhaps most jarringly though, Batman inexplicably forgets his reputation as shadowy vigilante by appearing at jungle parties.[17]

Clearly, Schumacher is not merely emulating Burton's visual paradigm for Batman's mythology but rather elaborating on it, adding another, somewhat unlooked-for ingredient: a more comedic, campy, and non-serious overtone which is even more robust than Burton's grotesque depiction of Joker in 1989. This process of "lightening" the structures that Burton had drenched in the noirish shadows started precisely with the 1995 *Batman Forever*, perfectly epitomizing that new camp noir aesthetic which sought to balance the campy, the cartoony, and the recent expressionistic iterations into one, genuinely explosive artistic mix. Schumacher himself admitted openly in Michael Singer's *Batman Forever. The Official Movie Book*: "I think Tim did a wonderful job with the other movies ... but to copy someone isn't really to flatter them. I think it was incumbent upon us to give our own version of the Batman legend, trying to incorporate some of the things Tim started, but also to give it a new, never-before-seen look" (1995: 12). Singer adds later: "The goal was to bring audiences a new concept of the Batman myth, shimmering with color, shadow, light and movement" (12).

If one were trying to find an apposite description of the camp noir scheme conceived by Joel Schumacher for his Batman duology, there is another term frequently highlighted by the director and numerous observers over the years: the "living comic book" experience. It follows the interpretations or intuitions of the film crew members, as most of them mention similar elements which produce "the living comic book" in which Schumacher was interested. According to Janet and Lee Batchlers—the screenwriters for *Batman Forever*—some of the fundamentals in Schumacher's mode of filmmaking were his obsession with color enhancement and the tenet of "lots of colors, lots of movement," which would make it possible to achieve comic book quality in a cinematic feature. In yet another insight, this time from Ve Neill—a make-up artist on *Forever*—Schumacher's own flamboyant presence was a key and potent factor, causing the film to be "more lighthearted ... and very colorful, and very upbeat and very broad."[18] One of the most crucial members of the crew, production designer Barbara Ling, added to the final style along these lines:

> The idea too is that you're staying within mainly night so neon becomes a very important element. And creating many influences of neon, the beautiful neon signs of the 20s and 30s, that would have really taken you the look that you see kind of a 42nd Street in old black and white photographs to what Tokyo has now which is wild graphics on giant proportions.[19]

The graphicness of those living comic books that both Schumacher's Batmen are was apparently explicitly demanded daily on the set: Nicole Kidman mentions "heightened reality," a byword commonly heard whilst filming *Batman Forever*,[20] and Barbara Ling corroborates that striving for the comic book feel: "We were very influenced by the comics ... which ... always had these wonderful color washes in the frames. In one panel, the wash would be red, and in the next scene, blue. That was very striking to us, and we felt that it was an important element to capture" (Singer 1995: 60). In fact, multiple catchphrases describing the "Schumacher look" are cited, including "post-apocalyptic expressionism ... giant graphic elements of graffiti, but all done in ultra-violet paint lit with incandescent lights" (Singer 1995: 69), visuals in the vein of "Frankenstein meets Las Vegas" (see Singer 1997: 54), and "psycho-disco" flavor (see Singer 1997: 57). Finally, Michael Gough (who played the faithful butler Alfred to both Tim Burton's and Joel Schumacher's versions of Bruce Wayne) should perhaps be credited with the most accurate characterization of that living comic book approach as an expansion of Burton's former artistic mannerisms: "Tim was more a psychological thriller and Joel is more a viewing thriller—an excitement to look at."[21] Akiva Goldsman endorses this notion, commenting that "Joel's style is very presentational and operatic."[22]

This visual thriller built around vibrant colors magnified by blasts of neon light, set in a post-apocalyptic expressionist landscape featuring oversized gargoyles and crooked alleyways winding between enormous skyscrapers translates into a genuine attempt at finding balance between the graphic absurdity deriving from camp imagery and the essential post-Burtonism with its taste for gothicized spaces. Mark S. Reinhart concludes that it ultimately brought about a complete divorce from reality due to its overwhelming penchant for "outrageously garish shades of magenta, orange and lime green. These colors did not seem to match up with the images of the dark, shadow-lined streets of Gotham City" (2013: 181). *Batman Forever*'s cinematographer Stephen Goldblatt noticed that that particular palette was anything but random: "Batman's are blues and purples and whites. Two-Face is red and magenta. The Riddler is green. … It really bangs out, and that's great about them. We're not trying to be subtle. I really liked it when Joel said from the beginning that he wanted the film to be operatic" (Singer 1995: 51). The fundamental problem lies in the very notion of Batman's accurate depiction: should it lean substantially towards the Dark Knight or be more inclusive and embrace the neon-lit, brighter presence that Schumacher wanted to bring to the fore? Thus, the real question is whether Schumacher achieved that overall comic book quality as he had intended, and also how could one appreciate his effort as a valuable feat of adapting the graphic exploits of cartoony superheroes? Despite Reinhart's reluctance towards Schumacher's attempt to un-darken the Dark Knight, which apparently failed due to poor choice of colors, other commentators underscore the different aesthetic yield that came with the director's effort to overcome the black-hued practical realism of Batman's character and environment.

In Kimberly Ann Owczarski's dissertation, in which she studied the Batman franchise in the light of modern conglomerate filmmaking, Schumacher's work is described as exaggeration-focused, as the duology attempts to mirror the director's taste for multilayered excess in the ecstatic portrayals of the protagonists and similarly overblown visuals (see Owczarski 2008: 270), which make it a "*Saturday Night Fever* on acid."[23] As a result, both Schumacher films evince the "living comic book on screen" approach, in which artistic overstatement is the prevalent factor: the colors are bedazzling, the movements and gestures of the characters theatrical, the camera angles are crooked, and the set designs declare that "nothing here is a normal world"[24] from the very opening seconds. In other words, Schumacher's formula for achieving this living comic book experience in a motion picture is to follow a slightly altered definition of the graphic medium introduced by Scott McCloud: while in McCloud's *Understanding Comics* comic book-ness may result from a strategy involving amplification through simplification, Schumacher's living comic book-ness is obtained by amplification through exaggeration, where every diegetic and non-diegetic element has to verge on invasive in its impact on the viewer's perception. Finally, the "neon" attribute defining Schumacher's Knight can be presumed to reflect the deliberate decision to take the Batman character out of his regular shadows and place him right in the center of this over-orchestrated and overdesigned setting so as to trespass this particular artistic taboo and create a Batman who can abandon his metaphorical dark cave, both visually and tonally.

To be fair, Joel Schumacher's Batmen are hardly the first to have attempted such an aggressive "redrawing" of a comic book in a feature film. The 1990s had none of the CGI which is widely used today to lend comic book quality to a motion picture, in adaptations such as Zack Snyder's *300* (2006) or Edgar Wright's *Scott Pilgrim vs the World* (2010). Still, a number of interesting productions actively pursued what Dru Jeffries calls "expressive intermediality," meaning "the presence of conventions associated with comics, both visual (e.g. caricature, particular use of line and color) and narrative (e.g. text captions, speech or thought balloons, onomatopeias, motion lines)" (2017: 23), and achieved an original form of stylistic remediation of the comic book into film, also referred to as transmedia style by, for instance, Drew Morton (see Morton 2017: 36). Schumacher films about Batman surely belong among those early efforts to find such a transmedia aesthetic, asserting directly that the world presented onscreen has no interest in any sort of psychological or artistic "toning down" of the inherent preference of comic books to amplify meanings or messages by simplifying them (although with Schumacher both the meanings and messages in his Batman flicks are simplified yet exaggerated by a never-ending march of vivid images and unsophisticated emotional cadence). An attempt akin to Schumacher's living comic book project may be found in another often-disregarded comic book film of the 1990s, namely Warren Beatty's *Dick Tracy* (1990), which shares many ground-breaking concepts of how to show a comic book on the screen with the later neon-Batman releases. The aesthetic aspect of *Dick Tracy* was comprehensively discussed by Michael Cohen in a detailed study of the 1990s cinematic underdog, in which the author made a number of worthwhile observations concerning Beatty's ideas for animating comic book panels. Regarding the most crucial artistic tools employed in that intriguing feature, Cohen uses the term "the aesthetic of artifice" to describe the film's expressive, comic book-based intermediality whose main premise is to "refuse to let the spectator forget this film is based on a comic. A strategy of 'cartooning' in *Dick Tracy* makes the choreography of character actions and behaviors implausible, and complements the 'aesthetic of artifice' in the production design" (2007: 20). Plus, multiple cinematic techniques were used to underscore the "artifice": 1) impracticality of the props, elaborate prosthetics of the characters, and cartoon-like make-up; 2) affected poses commonly assumed by characters; 3) blatant artificiality of set designs with theatrical lightning; 4) extensive application of consciously "uncinematic" production and postproduction methods, such as speeding-up character movement during fight scenes, frequent use of intra-frame editing instead of the more "acceptable" and genre-accurate inter-frame method; and finally 5) the now virtually iconic (for this specific iteration of Tracy) use of a diopter lens capable of providing a sharp focus on both the foreground and background elements to sustain the impression of seeing a single comic book frame on the screen.

    Cohen concludes his analysis by recognizing *Dick Tracy* to have been the result of simplification-through-amplification filmmaking rooted in comics, an unconventional comic book adaptation which strove to find a way to transmediation. *Dick Tracy*'s aesthetic of artifice was indeed implemented in Joel Schumacher's living comic book project since a number of Beatty's tricks may be seen in the neon Batmen as well. One of the most significant elements is the overall "impracticality" of Schumacher's visions; both *Batman Forever* and *Batman & Robin* open with elaborate scenes portraying the protagonists as they set out to fight evil. There is a long focus on the neon-lit Batmobile slowly coming up through the Batcave's floor—just to stand there for a minute in a glamorous shot is nothing more than a celebration of the image, a moment for the viewer to feast their eyes on the shiny, sinuous surface of a car. Similarly, the over-the-top costumes and gadgets of the superheroes—which Schumacher films are also notorious for—inclusive of the infamous white-themed "snow costumes" from *Batman & Robin*'s final fight with Arnold Schwarzenegger's Mr. Freeze exploit the look-over-use approach which aims to ensure visual thrill (as a visual thriller should), where watching a prop makes more sense than having it slowly introduced and explained. Schumacher's Batman films also boast make-up and costume design exaggerations, the most conspicuous of which is the pink facial burn prosthetic of Tommy Lee Jones's Two-Face and the LED-illuminated outfit of Mr. Freeze, which would have been pointless in practicality-oriented storytelling but do well in the artifice-centered agenda of the living comic book. Other noteworthy elements include the theatrical and highly contrived poses of Schumacher's heroes and villains, indicative of an obvious effort to obtain shots that make one think of a cartoon rather than reality. The impressive entrance of Val Kilmer's Batman in *Batman Forever* in the first few minutes shows the Neon Knight swirling on his Bat-rope down the street, his cape majestically floating back, whereas in the film's big highlight Batman intervenes at the neon-filled party hijacked by Two-Face, slowly falling down through a skylight in a shot celebrating the essence of the bat-like figure which descends in a slowed visual composition that lasts a good few seconds. The even more absurd scenes in Schumacher's duology, such as George Clooney's Batman swishing his cape to reveal the prostrate form of Mr. Freeze, prioritize the look of almost immobilized characters as in the comic book frame rather than continuing the cinematic movement of the preceding dynamic chase sequence. The final view of Gotham City—an urban space dominated by unbelievable, overgrown gargoyles and Greek-like male sculptures, neon-sprayed alleys, and street corners, the thoroughly abstract locations and cartoonish landscapes, e.g., The Riddler's lair built to resemble his brain-draining invention called "The Box," or the local observatory shaped like a giant statue holding the telescope dome—in no way depict any "practical" structure. All such sets and places follow the doctrine of artifice, creating spaces that offer an exciting backdrop to equally nonsensical motions and actions of the protagonists, in which looks trump making sense. This is splendidly illustrated by Robin's visually compelling entrance during the initial museum showdown with Mr. Freeze (in *Batman & Robin*), where the young hero's motorcycle crashes through the door leaving Robin's emblem-shaped hole; there is no other point to it other than delivering yet another "visual thrill."

Schumacher's Neon Knight lives in this strange realm of absurd geography, surrounded by blinding colors and lights, cartoonish behavior and avails himself of a constantly growing number of gadgets and vehicles, far in excess of a respected Dark Knight persona. Still, does this overhaul of Batman's mythology really damage the visual integrity of the character too much? Is it indeed embarrassing to see a Batman who inhabits a land of unpractical yet visually compelling and teeming locations in which he is presented as a mythical figure with all the awe-inspiring trappings of a superhero as opposed to an urban law enforcer? The thing is that even despite the general disapproval arising from the thematic aftermath of the Neon Knight—which will be covered later—Schumacher's living comic book drew a striking dividing line between the viewers who pleaded for a mature, i.e., less operatic and cartoony Batman story, and the viewers who were genuinely amazed by the unique ability of those films to make every single image exciting. Just as Tegan O'Neil advised:

> Please, do not take my word for it: just watch it. Turn the volume off if you need. Look at the color. Lean into the baroque excess. Enjoy the scenery being chewed like the crew refused to feed the actors and hid sandwiches in the wall. The cinematography! Every inch of every frame has been composed almost to obsequiousness. It is, frankly, a marvel – it anticipates every excess of the digital color era.[25]

The fact is that for Schumacher each and every shot should be exaggerated and each and every scene should ensure a blood-pumping transition to another highly energized shot or scene. Schumacher appears to be overly dramatic and representation-focused—as Akiva Goldsman noted—but he is very consistent in this type of "dramatic cartoon" filmmaking. Take for instance Bruce Wayne's somewhat abrupt entry into Dr. Chase Meridian's office as they meet for the first time in *Batman Forever*. The scene starts with a classic shot of Wayne walking the down the hallway with the camera slowly shifting to Dutch angle, while shrill screaming of a woman is heard. A quick succession of shots showing Wayne struggling with the doors to Meridian's office—with Dutch angle throughout—ends with him breaking through the obstacle just to see the doctor—all safe and sound—exercising with a punching bag, while the composition of the scene reverts from Dutch angle as if the "crooked" heroic persona of Wayne in action were coming back to a more "straight" public presence.

The living comic book adopted by Schumacher translates into an almost thoroughly immersive cinema experience—in which there is no particular interest in cultivating the substance of the story but extensive effort goes into enhancing the audial and visual ingredients of cinema. In addition to the visuals, an essential role belongs to Elliot Goldenthal's equally operatic score and the simplified-through-exaggeration manner of composition. The music written for both Schumacher films fluctuates constantly between the experimental and absurdly atonal compositions like *Nygma Variations (An Ode to Science)* from *Batman Forever* to the more uplifting and heroic tune of Batman's main theme, which is far more inspiring and pulse-raising than Danny Elfman's moody, atmospheric, and mystical pieces in Tim Burton's films. There is interesting inspiration behind Goldenthal's score, as the composer explained:

> I was trying to remember myself as like a little child playing with a maybe a little Batman toy. I was thinking what are the children singing? They sing their own scores. If you look and watch kids play they're composing their own music.[26]

Clearly, Schumacher's overall simplification-through-exaggeration technique was at play in this department as well, as the musical component was to be as informative, exciting, and as bare-bones as possible. Even so, Goldenthal's music—widely regarded as inferior to the much-appreciated contribution of

Elfman's—appears to dovetail perfectly with the heroic narrative (along with other classics, such as John Williams' *Superman* theme or Alan Silvestri's *The Avengers* theme), as it draws prominently from the source material of heroic scores by—as Matthew David Young demonstrates—developing variations on the military themes (see Young 2013). Goldenthal's leitmotif—more uplifting and less eerie than the Batman main theme by Elfman—constitutes another token of the Schumacher-driven shift towards the living comic book experience, where all requisite qualities were amplified to make those features a multisensory thrill. This interpretation of Joel Schumacher's Neon Knight in the light of the aesthetic values he espoused underscores the paradigm of optical and compositional exaggeration, by means of which the depiction of Batman as the Dark Knight could be realigned to obtain a more luminous variation. As it is, Schumacher's involvement in the Batman franchise in 1995 marked a significant change with respect to Burton's earlier interpretation that produced the Noir-tmare Knight. Instead of an expressionistic Christmas Carol, the audience received a psychedelic explosion of light-and-dark contrasts, which honored the achievement of the previous films but also overcame their exceedingly monochromatic mood. As a result, Schumacher certainly succeeded in exploring the living comic book concept to the full, thus exposing an obvious truth about the main character that many refused to acknowledge, the truth of his comic book roots and largely unrestricted visual possibilities which went far beyond the limited realistic approach. That particular director's version of a superhero film as a visual thriller directly drew on the 1960s Camp Knight's colorful vividness, only to elaborate on it and brighten Batman lore with the omnipresent incandescence of the costumes, gadgets, and landscapes, as well as accomplish a neon-lit shift in filmmaking towards the celebration of artifice. Bearing this in mind, one can recall the final riddle of *Batman Forever*—"I see without seeing. To me, darkness is as clear as daylight. What am I?"—through which Schumacher describes the hybrid of darkness and daylight that he tried to achieve. However, this attempt to lighten Gotham City and its heroic inhabitants entailed a much more significant consequence of having the Neon Knight thus materialized. Once again, this should be attributed to a tendency originating with Schumacher, whereby one looks past the "norm" to envision a psychologically "lightened"

Batman as well. In a conversation with John C. Tibbetts, the director admitted that the most iconic image from his first take on Batman in *Batman Forever*—the spectacular Bat-signal within a question mark projected in the sky just before the climax of the movie—"questions Bruce Wayne and Batman's entire existence and he poses for him a choice at the end of the movie."[27] In line with Schumacher's intentions, that symbolic emblem may be read as both a strictly diegetic nod towards Bruce Wayne's quandary of whether to accept or reject his dual personality, and a much more meta-textual question about what Batman really is or can be (or when Batman stops being Batman) and what makes the Batman icon truly forever?

2.3 The Lite Knight rises: The troublesome case of plastic figures, virtual grappling hooks, and rubber nipples

While the 1992 image of the hideous Penguin emerging from a sewer with dark saliva dripping from his mouth or the sight of Catwoman stretching sensuously in her skin-tight costume had troubled the licensees and concerned parents, it was clear from the very first day of hiring Joel Schumacher that one specific target group had to be satisfied to ensure the film's future success—the toy manufacturers and burger chains, whose endorsement would probably restore the faith in Batman among America's parents. There is no better example of this new alliance between the merchandise producers and the filmmakers—a bond of trust that Tim Burton's team had considerably undermined—than the leading commercial aired in 1995 as part of a McDonald's campaign, the chief attraction of which was limited *Batman Forever*-themed glasses featuring the main characters from the movie. As if the very first line from the actual film was not enough to convey a new communion between the onscreen fantasy and a real-life restaurant, the commercial put extra emphasis on the fact that the Batman franchise is an integral element in their food range. The short clip sees a typical McDonald's worker asked by the manager to go to the storage room and find some straws. As the young woman is looking for them, she accidently comes across a secret entrance to the Batcave, located just beneath an outlet. As the inadvertent trespasser navigates the fantastic scenery, she happens to see Batman himself posing for the collectible glasses as they are manufactured in his crime-fighting headquarters. The heroine subsequently leaves abruptly and dramatically shuts the storage room door, only to recall that she had forgotten the straws her boss asked her to bring. Fortunately, a helping hand emerges as the Caped Crusader instantly provides the product needed. Apparently absurd, the short clip—considering the main concerns of the film studio and the primary task entrusted to Joel Schumacher as the director of the feature—conclusively attests to the renewed tie between the fictional vigilante and broadly understood consumerism, symbolized by the iconic logo of the golden arches.

Over the years following the premieres of both *Batman Forever* and *Batman & Robin*, it became something of a mantra to speak of the Schumacher movies as strictly commercially driven or denounce them as two-hour-long cinematic commercials which advertised non-cinematic products. Tim Hanley puts it succinctly: "Directed by Joel Schumacher, *Batman Forever* was colorful and somewhat silly, ideal for action figures and other merchandise for young fans" (2017: 167). Certainly, Schumacher's Batmen are just that to some degree— invasive to the senses, those loud spectacles undoubtedly launched a vast range of items to accompany the first 1995 feature, easily surpassing the estimated $750 million earned in merchandise by *Batman Returns*. Over time, the merchandise associated with Schumacher's work saw decreasing interest due to its firmly unconventional form and disputable outcome. Nevertheless, even the most obscure and problematic instances accentuated the toyetic nature of Schumacher's productions, which made an effort to establish the presence of the equally unconventional Neon Knight through significant Cute or Toy Knight components. In other words, when examining the "trespassive" bias of Schumacher's approach towards the Batman franchise and the overall feel of the "official" cinematic Batman under Schumacher, it may be worthwhile to consider the peripheral themes or secondary texts here, spanning action figures, video games, and, eventually, the intense dispute concerning the impact of the "rubber nipples" on Batman's "seriousness." These latter tropes reflect the unusual but certainly novel understanding of how Batman may be interpreted in any given medium.

The already cited Dan Fleming observed in his study of play involving movie merchandise that the very act of reimagining a toy as a post-spectacle object necessitated consent to grant the new spectacle-owners some sort of control over the original narrative. Fleming notes that "these new narrative contexts had multiple narrative possibilities deliberately built into them from the beginning. With early established teams of characters and basic story structures that would generate endless plots around the characters, children could certainly watch and read plenty of given examples, but were also being encouraged to extend those with their own variations" (1996: 104). The users and the producers of such spectacle-related toys were increasingly aware of this fact, which is eloquently exemplified by the 1990s Batman films and the action figures and playsets manufactured by Kenner (beginning with the 1990 range called *The Dark Knight Collection*). Their products duplicated the cinematic counterparts, perhaps superficially at times, but with every new film they expanded on points in the plot to afford more open scenarios than the original narrative. This is discernible in the essential range of Kenner's action figures following the respective "waves" of *Batman Forever* and *Batman & Robin*:

- the *Batman Forever* line eventually consisted of twenty-one basic stand-alone figures, with the initial Wave 1 set including character variations such as Blast Cape Batman, Fireguard Batman, Hydro Claw Robin, Manta Ray Batman, Night Hunter Batman, Sonar Sensor Batman, Street Biker Robin, The Riddler, Transforming Bruce Wayne, Transforming Dick Grayson, and Two-Face;
- similarly, the *Batman & Robin* premiere was accompanied by thirty-two basic single action-figure packs; Wave 1 comprised some more remote variants of the heroes and villains featured in the film: Bane, Batgirl, Battle Gear Bruce Wayne, Heat Scan Batman, Hover Attack Batman, Iceblast Mr. Freeze, Iceboard Robin, Jungle Venom Poison Ivy, and Razor Skate Robin.

Given the observations made by Dan Fleming, the action figures listed above undoubtedly capitalized on the idea of products that referenced specific film events and, simultaneously, offered potential starting points to expand a given scene or plot. Each of the Wave 1 figures from both movies clearly follows this pattern; for instance, the Fireguard Batman from the *Batman Forever* line (Batman in fireproof armor) draws on the scene in which the maniacal Two-Face tries to burn the hero in an underground assault (Batman escapes thanks to the fireproof properties of his outfit). The Manta Ray Batman, with expanded deep-diving gear, is inspired by one of the final scenes from the movie's climax, in which Batman struggles briefly with Two-Face's henchmen underwater and rescues Robin (whose underwater variant—Hydro Claw Robin—was also offered). Much the same happens with *Batman & Robin*: Kenner's Hover Attack Batman and Iceboard Robin figures included a peculiar type of hoverboard, vaguely reminiscent of the 1997 *Batman & Robin*'s spectacular surfboard flight from Mr. Freeze's rocket exploding over Gotham City. The same pattern is observed with every action figure associated with both features, while some may actually serve as testimonies or mementos of the removed or reinterpreted material. For instance, the Night Flight Batman from *Batman Forever*'s Wave 3 is something of a reference to a deleted scene featuring a giant man-bat creature, recycled for the figure as a bat-shaped flying suit which gives the hero a truly gothic look. The 1997 Ambush Attack Batman wears a vibrant green costume which may bring to mind the final confrontation with Uma Thurman's Poison Ivy in her plant-controlled lair, where Batman has to fight with the mutant flora. Every single figure produced in conjunction with both blockbusters clearly evinces what Tyrone Keyes—the design team leader for Kenner in 1997— demurely admitted: "We took some liberties" (*Batman & Robin. The Official Souvenir Magazine* 1997: 63). Indeed, in terms of design and potential use, the toys did try to not duplicate the appearance of onscreen characters but treated them as points of departure for further dramatic themes or simply inspiration for cool-looking outfits which would engage the imagination of children to expand on the actual narrative.

Within the Neon Knight iteration, the commercial element manifesting in the action figures may be considered to have nurtured the process of cutening the erstwhile Dark Knight image, given Kenner's strategic-level decision to avoid the most "traditional" representations of Batman (even those depicted in Schumacher's films) for the sake of offering more and more colorful and glitzy plastic versions of the hero. In fact, hardly any item from the *Batman Forever* and *Batman & Robin* merchandise lines can be called true-to-screen. One could perhaps name the so-called Panther Suit and the Sonar Suit from the 1995 film, which were recreated without major modifications in the Sonar Sensor Batman and the Guardians of Gotham two-pack set, with Batman and Robin largely as they looked in *Batman Forever*'s finale. This absence of continued representation is even more acute with Schumacher's second Batman: a Batman figure as shown in the film is nowhere to be found, with the probable exception of the fairly far-fetched Hover Attack Batman, based on the standard movie costume, and the 1997 Guardians of Gotham two-pack, in which the metallic armors of Batman and Robin imitate the ice-themed outfits from the concluding sequences. In line with Schumacher's underlying art concept, it would be legitimate to claim that the trespassing agenda resonates even in the domain of merchandise, focused as it was on commercial outcomes, as the design of toys created for the franchise chose to overlook the "traditional" Batman embodiment in favor of aesthetic variation. Thus, Batman's plastic likenesses obtained increasingly brightened tones and apparel which departed substantially from the essential darks and grays. Schumacher was actually involved to some degree in the early stages of toy development, and that army of green, purple, blue, red, brown, or purple hero figures may be suggestive of the director's indirect acknowledgement that the un-darkened Batman he envisioned takes root elsewhere. Interestingly, the routine avoidance of any classical design in the toys Kenner created for Schumacher's films is often mentioned today by numerous fans, who vividly recall the lack of a "proper" Batman action figure during the *Batman Forever* and *Batman & Robin* craze. One of the podcasters of the YouTube channel Superhero Stuff You Should Know reminisced about the Schumacher-related toy range: "These are pretty cool but it did bother me as a kid when I would go to the store and like look at these, I had a bunch of *Batman Forever* figures but it was like why can't I just find Batman in that black costume? That's what I wanted."[28] As cruel as it would have sounded for many of the young fans back then, it was a major element supporting Schumacher's overall intention to deliver his Neon Knight persona, whose best offscreen equivalent would probably be the Neon Armor Batman—featured in both the 1995 and the 1997 lines—portraying the Knight in the eponymous luminescent suit: a look that was in multiple senses lighter than the visualization of the dark detective.

Presuming that the entirety of the commercial products surrounding Schumacher's Batmen were in keeping with his design to overcome the traditional appearance of the Dark Knight as well as the character's narrative and/or aesthetic schemes, the action figures would qualify among the many other popular products which proved highly controversial due to unexpected mechanics implemented in that Batman-related offers. In a similar way to the toys, concerns about forcing Batman into an unwanted and apparently unproductive domain of brand-building were provoked by various video games drawing on Schumacher's Batman duology. In the opinion of many gamers, they are probably the worst attempts to add elements of ergodic entertainment to Batman's exploits. Both *Batman Forever* and *Batman & Robin* were accompanied by game releases developed for popular gaming consoles and computer systems available in the 1990s. The main game to accompany *Batman Forever* was essentially the same product formatted for the 8- and 16-bit platforms—including Super Nintendo Entertainment System and Sega Genesis/Mega Drive, handheld devices from both producers, i.e., Nintendo Game Boy and Sega Game Gear, as well as personal computers running MS-DOS. In addition, the main publisher involved, Acclaim Entertainment, released another title for arcade platforms, also developed by Probe Entertainment. The classic iteration of the *Batman Forever* video game for home systems was a beat'em-up, an undemanding, side-scrolling fighting game—a "button-masher" as some fans called it: one had to use the "hit" button very frequently during gameplay that consisted of wandering through every level to vanquish all the enemies and/or complete specific tasks (such as freeing bank hostages on Game Boy's Level 1, which referenced the first minutes of the 1995 film in which Val Kilmer's Batman saves a bank guard, or respectively SNES/Genesis first level with Batman battling an army of the Arkham Asylum's lunatic inmates, which is loosely based on the scripted and filmed—but eventually cut—opening sequence of Two-Face's escape from this psychiatric facility for dangerous criminals). The game also featured minor RPG elements, limited to the strategy of selecting the arsenal (e.g., the Bat Bolas or Slippery Goo) for a particular location, and offered a cooperation mode, with two players able to play as Batman and Robin at one time, but the option was available only on the SNES and Genesis platforms. The arcade version—adapted later for the Sony PlayStation and Sega Saturn consoles—had a different quality altogether. Still a beat'em-up, the game was much more elaborate due to its eye-catching settings and exhausting pace with swarms of endlessly charging enemies suddenly popping out from behind elements of the landscape; on top of this, there was the dizzying presentation of the character's power-up, filling the screen with stroboscopic extravaganza. Both versions—as well as the 1997 *Batman & Robin* sandbox adventure game—deserve a more detailed discussion, therefore the following paragraphs will focus on the first interactive version of *Batman Forever*, since it epitomizes the concerns about, as well as revealing some encouraging aspects of, the attempts to "play-up" the Neon Knight in the Schumacher era.

Since its first release in 1995, the basic virtual adaptation of *Batman Forever* maintains its rather regrettable status of one of the worst superhero games of all time and, frankly, one of the worst games in general. Subsequent generations of gamers and reviewers consistently cite the same shortcomings of this product, widely known for its rather unattractive visuals and discouraging appeal, which may sound ironic given the original criticism of the style-over-substance approach in the motion picture on which that particular game was based. More recent reports concerning the game, published, for instance, by the YouTube channel Movies to Video Games Reviews, succinctly restate its incontrovertible main disadvantages: "Some of the worst play controls and play mechanics ever found in game. Using gadgets, fighting and navigating through levels is a real chore. This game is not fun at any point. Its overtly difficult, has horrible controls, awful level designs and all you do is fight the same enemies over and over again."[29] Admittedly, over the years *Batman Forever* has gained a reputation for one of the most frustrating gameplays ever created, mostly due to the very unintuitive and unnecessarily complicated system of controlling the character, which makes even the basic movements a difficult task. It has become something of a standing joke among the gamers that the very first stage of the opening level is an unmitigated conceptual nightmare, where the main challenge is not merely to overcome the incoming enemies but to master a simple gadget which is nonetheless vital for the rest of the game: the notorious Bat grappling hook, which helps Batman or Robin reach a structure or object above. Unfortunately, the counter-intuitive combination of buttons required to use the rope—"Select" and "Up" in a very precise order—is exceedingly confusing, while the level gives very little indication about where the grappling hook should be used to get to a higher floor; so at first the game may seem "unplayable" as the player is simply stuck at the end of the first hallway.

Despite its rather disappointing final form, *Batman Forever* for SNES and Sega Genesis was extensively advertised in 1995. The main element in its advertising campaign was a short television commercial showing a few snippets from the actual game and a dramatic micronarrative about Batman and Robin—both presented as stuntmen in costumes as in the film—catching a fugitive from a prison. This quite effective and protreptic sequence was supplemented with the standard recital of the most exciting features of the game, at least according to the advertisers: a chance to team up as Batman and Robin, find many hidden surprises, see incredible 3D graphics and explore over eighty levels with 125 awesome attacks. The advert culminated with a catchy tune and a chorus: "You can run, there's no escape. You can hide, that's his fate. He can fight with all his might and never win. When good battle's evil, the real game begins." Given the actual quality of the game, such advertising material is even more misleading when it turns out that the alleged highlights are effectively compromised by the awkward and underdeveloped mechanics. However, the inferior experience of the controls notwithstanding, the premise of the game deserves some sort of recognition, if only in view of the developer's intentions attempt to deliver *Batman Forever* as an ergodic tie-in to popular cinematic content based on an interesting idea, making it possible to enrich previous Batman-related games by surpassing their generic and mechanical settings with unexpected input.

With both Tim Burton's Batman films, efforts were made to translate the diegetic cinematic works into interactive games for the third and fourth generation of home consoles; *Batman* and *Batman Returns* inspired around ten different attempts at a virtual interpretation of the original films. Essentially, all contemporary game systems received at least one adaptation of either feature, most of which followed the pattern of action-oriented side-scrolling gameplay with the occasional modifications available with individual platforms. The list includes *Batman* (1989) for Amiga, Amstrad CPC, Apple II, Commodore 64, MS-DOS, ZX Spectrum, *Batman* (1989) for Nintendo Entertainment System, *Batman* (1990) for GameBoy, *Batman* (1990) for Sega Genesis/

Mega Drive, *Batman Returns* (1992) for Game Gear, Genesis, MS-DOS, NES, Atari Lynx, and *Batman Returns* (1993) for Super NES, Master System, Sega CD, Amiga. Importantly, each of the above would have to be analyzed on its own merits, since the 1989 *Batman* for NES is drastically different from the 1990 *Batman* for Sega Genesis or the 1989 handheld Game Boy version due to distinct game and console engines, as well as completely different sets of aesthetic and controlling paradigms. In relation to the aforementioned *Batman Forever* game for home systems, it may be crucial to highlight the most iconic and fairly universally acclaimed of the previous ergodic extensions to Batman films, i.e., the 1989 *Batman* for NES and 1993 *Batman Returns* for SNES, which even today stand out as the most successful renderings into the 8- and 16-bit environment.

As already noted, both could be classified as a side-scrolling action game genre-wise, meaning that the gamer's main task is to move forward (or in this case towards the right side of the screen) and eliminate the enemies trying to attack Batman's virtual avatar. However, these particular attempts enhance the straightforward formula with new possibilities for exploring the story worlds adapted from the movies. In the NES *Batman*, this "unconventional" component involves a more platform-oriented movement within each level, as the traditional left-to-right mechanics are supplemented with a range of possible vertical motions, which necessarily include abilities such as wall jumping. For many experienced gamers, this particular addition reflects an attempt to combine classic side-scrolling with a *Ninja Gaiden*-like experience, as a result of which the gameplay requires the user to show some more refined skill to be able to complete each level, which was more than a simple beat'em-up could offer. The SNES *Batman Returns*, on the other hand, represents a classic instance of the latter, with the character of Batman in the center of the left-to-right screen journey peppered with tons of diversified enemies, including the infamous Red Triangle Circus gang led by the menacing Penguin. Though a candid throwback to other classic titles, such as the *Final Fight* series, *Batman Returns* has been praised for the quality of its specific components: it is often described as exceedingly satisfying, considering Batman's considerable set of skills and punches and the compelling sound design, including the yells of the goons and musical cues. All in all, it quite successfully introduced elements reminiscent of the scenes, events, and even the land- and soundscapes from the movies into the console adaptation.

In the context of these two particularly well-remembered efforts to translate Batman's cinematic adventures of the 1990s into tie-in video games, the *Batman Forever* game may be seen as even more troublesome and unworthy of an any critical attention. As noted previously, the final outcome was substandard but, overall, one could appreciate the official *Batman Forever* video game as a multiplatform project relying on the premise of implementing a well-known pattern in a Batman-centered gameplay (just as the 1989 *Batman* for NES drew on the game characteristics of *Ninja Gaiden*), specifically the fighting mode from the popular *Mortal Kombat* series. It is by no means an accident that the famous arcade fighting game developed and launched by Midway Games in 1992 was adapted only a year later for all home systems—SNES, Sega Genesis, Game Boy, and Game Gear—by Acclaim, the same company responsible for the release of the *Batman Forever* game. Its final form demonstrates rather obvious borrowings from Midway's hit arcade. The mechanics of the game is the first and most conspicuous element: *Batman Forever* features *Mortal Kombat*-like gameplay, including the elaborate fighting styles of each enemy, who had been much more predictable in the side-scrolling, platform, and beat'em-up iterations accompanying the previous Batman films. It is also noteworthy that the characters from the Batman narrative resemble *Mortal Kombat* protagonists, as the developers of *Batman Forever* relied on the motion capture technology which Midway had used to render onscreen figures as animated sprites, producing a fairly impressive visual outcome with 16-bit gaming consoles. The results of the somewhat unexpected marriage between the two not entirely compatible game settings were disastrous, but the effort of venturing further afield and developing a Batman-dedicated tie-in game with novel characteristics deserves at least modest recognition. Although the infamous *Batman Forever* game is still ranked among the worst action games ever, a number of critics have recently begun to re-examine that strange conceptual and mechanical hybrid in view of its bold foray into uncharted territory:

> When it came to bringing *Batman Forever* to consoles and handhelds, things took a downward slide as Acclaim took over development duties and tried to

make a game that was part *Mortal Kombat*, part side-scrolling action game, a mix that's about as volatile as it sounds but as *MK* was one of, if not the most popular game at the time, I can at least see why they tried to trick people into thinking the two would be at least somewhat similar.[30]

Both the plastic and virtual renderings of the content in *Batman Forever* continue to be rightfully recognized as genuinely problematic or simply misguided, having failed to deliver the "expected" commercial objects, such as classic molds and costume designs for the Batman action figures or a competently made video game that would be enjoyable and—even more essentially— simply playable. However, in a broader context these two cases appear to share a common trait concerned with the general concept of "Schumacher's Batman." As already observed, merchandise in the shape of action figures and the video game projects arguably constituted supplementary material in constructing the Neon Knight as an audacious variation that goes way beyond the most commonly accepted versions of the Dark Knight. Instead, what one got was an odd range of nonsensical products, like the rainbow-colored Batman figures with absurd gadgets or a console game that besides it crippled engine was just a bizarre experiment in expanding the scope of gameplay. And yet, those two instances serve as non-diegetic ingredients in Schumacher's version of the Neon Knight as, once again, a variation may be technically flawed or aesthetically objectionable but is still a counterproposal to the most obvious conceptions of Batman, even in the strictly commercial settings. In any case, that peculiar set of confusing toys and deficient game designs is a secondary issue to the much more unsettling choices Joel Schumacher made with respect to the movies, accomplishing what is widely considered the most incongruent cinematic portrayal of the Dark Knight, who thus transformed into the Lite Knight.

As the title of this chapter suggests, the triad of the most often criticized aspects of Schumacher's Batman embodiment is epitomized by three elements that many find to be the most accurate metaphors of his overall vision: the plastic figures (denoting the immoderate marketing and merchandise), virtual punches and grappling hooks (referencing the underwhelming quality of the video games originating with the films), and, finally, the most notorious of all, the conspicuous rubber nipples on Batman's movie outfits, which countless critics of Schumacher have cited over the years as a blatant act of "misunderstanding" the character. Joel Schumacher would explain the rationale behind his artistic choice on many occasions; it was an attempt to forge an onscreen presence of Batman as a continuation of the antique representations of immaculate naked bodies and male torsos. This, however, will not be the main concern of this section, as it may be more productive and innovative to determine what that particular visual manifestation of Batman could have possibly contributed to the character as such, instead of focusing on the much discussed oversexualization with a strong homosexual undertone. This specific aspect of Schumacher's interpretation—the inclusion of corporeal detail—circles back to our central question concerning the limited capacity to accept distinct variations or singular interpretations of a beloved fictional character. In Batman's case, there is a large repertory of presumed conventions that an "acceptable" interpretation should follow to be respected as "accurate." Apart from the already discussed properties like the color palette or the general "mood" of a Batman-centered aesthetic, there is an element which raises objections given the Dark Knight visual paradigm of the hero, for whom prominent rubber nipples are a direct attack on the character's somber appeal.

Still, the real question is not *whether* Batman should have visible nipples on his costume but for *what reason*. The undisputable rejection of the mere possibility that such anatomical detail is featured in the hero's costume evinces the allegiance of the most dedicated fans to the principles and standards which entail a limited range of possible portrayals of Batman, in keeping with the "canonical" interpretation that favors the traditional Dark Knight iteration. With regards to the specific act of emphasizing that unorthodox detail of Batman's appearance, it may be crucial to understand the reasoning behind such an artistic choice as opposed to its correctness, dictated by more or less flexible notions of the character. Consequently, Schumacher's problematic rubber nipples constitute an act of cultural and artistic trespassing, which violate the constraints of Batman's representation as well as the more universal imagery of an action hero in popular media. Thus, the "queering" aspect of Schumacher's Batman does not revolve around sexual connotations or homosexual fantasy that needs to be exposed and dissected; it is all about the progressive challenge with which Schumacher confronts the portrayal of the male superhero in general.

Crucially, one has to approach Schumacher's Batman as an element of a broader question about the visualization of male and female characters in popular culture of the 1980s and 1990s, so as to eventually account for the rubber nipples. Considering the overall strategy of portraying masculine heroes in mass-produced visual media such as film and comics, Christina Adamou observes:

> To be male is not to be "sexed"; to be "sexed" is always a way of becoming particular and relative, and males within this system participate in the form of the universal person, while for Foucault the body is not "sexed" in any significant sense prior to its determination within a discourse through which it becomes invested with an "idea" of natural or essential sex. The body gains meaning within discourse only in the context of power relations.
> (2011: 96)

The very act of "sexualization" to explicitly manifest one's sexual attributes (e.g., by means of nipples), or used as a technical measure to "capture" specific traits of a sexualized character (as conceived by Laura Mulvey with respect to cinematic voyeurism), translates directly—as Adamou explains—into character building informed strictly by the polarity of dominance and subordination, in which the alleged manly (super)hero has to be the dominant figure, i.e., he cannot be made "visible" by means of the overtly sexualized attributes or details typical of the (super)hero's love interest, who substantially depends on her savior. This particular logic is perfectly evinced in the culture and cult of the 1980s and 1990s action genre, whose main protagonists are masculine but not as sexualized as their female companions who, even though similarly athletic, demonstrate visible sexual attributes in their tight costumes. In all likelihood, the best material to explore the issue are the popular American superhero comics created by major artists of the 1990s, such as Jim Lee, Mike Deodato, Rob Liefeld, and Todd McFarlane, who were quite notorious for exploiting that approach in the popular DC and Marvel series such as *Wonder Woman*, *Thor*, and *X-Men*. A strong opposition between the physically attractive male characters with excessive muscle and sexually attractive female characters with overabundant erotic appeal shaped a general landscape for a similar division in portraying both genders in any form of popular fiction in the 1990s, including even animated shows for children such as *Teenage Mutant Ninja Turtles*, where the female protagonist who accompanies the turtles, reporter April O'Neil, displays a tempting cleavage.

This striking contrast between Schumacher's conceptually and graphically sexualized frivolous Neon Knight and the dominant model of Batman as the 1990s Dark Crusader and his graphic companions can be seen vividly by looking at the actual content of the Batman-related comic books published in 1995 and 1997 around the premieres of both Schumacher's movies as well as the overall vibe of Batman's graphic exploits throughout the 1990s, significantly exploring the "dark," ergo "male," elements of the Dark Knight's mythos. And so in June 1995, the month that *Batman Forever* hit American screens on June 16, new fans of the character (possibly inspired by the film) could actually face a disturbing dissonance by flicking through the Batman comics, as the main titles back then had basically nothing to do with the neon aesthetic of the actual motion picture. Instead, the most important Batman comic book magazines of that time—*Batman, Shadow of the Bat*, and *Legends of the Dark Knight*—were presenting stories such as *Black Spider: A Web of Scars* (*Batman* no. 519) by Doug Moench and Kelly Jones, introducing a new antagonist to the series known as the titular Black Spider in a noir-driven setting magnified by the characteristic hyper-expressionistic style of Jones's artwork. In the 72nd issue of *The Legends of the Dark Knight*, in a storyline entitled *Werewolf* by James Robinson and John Watkiss, Gotham's hero was portrayed in yet another horror-themed narrative facing the savage Wolfman himself. And finally in the 39th episode of the *Shadow of the Bat* series, Alan Grant and Kevin Walker were confronting Batman with a zombie-like figure of Solomon Grundy in once again a rather moody hardboiled detective/thriller story, *Solomon Grundy: One Night in Slaughter Swamp* with Grundy as an additional horror-like monster in the Batman's rouges catalog. Schumacher's more campy Batman was most certainly not the same Batman that one would find in the DC Comic's portfolio in 1995 with the leading graphic interpretation of the character seen more as a shadowy figure and not the full-blown hero that the Gotham's citizens could cheerfully welcome, like in *Batman Forever*'s

Nygmatech heist scene with one of the guests pointing towards Batman breaking through the roof with an ecstatic: "Batman! Yeah!"

A similar thing can be observed in June 1997—the month that *Batman & Robin*'s premiered on June 20—which exemplified perhaps an even more astonishing contrast between the seemingly happy-go-lucky portrayal of George Clooney's exploits as Batman in his chase for an ice-pun-delivering Schwarzenegger as Mr. Freeze with his toyetic costume and the actual content of Batman's comics like *Batman* no. 543 by Doug Moench and Kelley Jones, telling a chilling story of a new murderer in Gotham known as Faceless whose main agenda was to impersonate his poor victims through elaborate disguises. *Batman: The Long Halloween*, however, published in June 1997, illustrates even more perfectly this parting of ways between Schumacher's films and Batman's comics clearly uninterested in following the Neon Knight's more queer idea for the character but rather intensifying once again this Dark Knight's agenda instead. June 1997 marked the seventh issue of this acclaimed and widely celebrated miniseries by Jeph Loeb and Tim Sale, the ultimate Batman detective story highly influenced by the noir novels by Raymond Chandler and mob drama classics like Mario Puzo's *The Godfather*, making yet another detour from the campiness of *Batman & Robin* into a much more serious epic about Gotham's criminal underworld.

And even after the specific periods of June 1995 and June 1997 it is obvious that the graphic Batman and Schumacher's Batman were following different conceptual paths, with the comic book series clearly more interested in Batman as the Dark Knight persona, both visually and thematically. It is significant after all that, shortly before the premiere of *Batman & Robin*, the comic book image of Batman was marked by the revolutionary 1996 four-issue miniseries by Mark Waid and Alex Ross called *Kingdome Come*, a dystopian vision of the future for the DC Comics' universe with Batman as a much older yet still superbly capable mastermind taking a stand in a growing war between the "classic" heroes and the new generation of crimefighters. As Geoff Klock rightfully admits, *Kingdome Come* serves as yet another "revisionary narrative" for the superhero genre alongside Frank Miller's *The Dark Knight Returns* with a symbolic epilogue given here by Waid and Ross including the DC's Big Three—Superman, Batman, and Wonder Woman—visiting a superhero-themed restaurant modeled as "Planet Hollywood for superheroes, which includes memorabilia from the comic books, the Batman television show, George Reeves' Superman serial, and *Superfriends*" (Klock 2002: 97), suggesting the necessity of moving on with the sentimental and straightforward versions of heroes and not cherishing them like in Schumacher's Batman. And finally, can there really be a more significant act given by Schumacher himself in this process of removing Batman outside the dominant setting of 1990s comics than the director's treatment of Bane, the iconic Batman's villain of the XXth century's last decade in Batman comics, as the main antagonist of the groundbreaking storyline *Knightfall* starting in April 1993 and his standing as the one rogue that successfully broke Batman both mentally and physically? Created by Chuck Dixon and Graham Nolan, Bane can be seen as the ultimate creation of the 1990s comic book aesthetic: the master villain portrayed as a wrestler or even a luchador-like type of excessively muscled brute with a hairy chest seen clearly through his rather skimpy shirt and posing a real challenge to Batman as an equal to him in both intelligence and martial arts skill. As Graham Nolan himself admitted:

> The parameters for him had to be that he must be the intellectual and physical equal of Batman, that it would be believable that he could beat Batman and injure him badly enough to put him out of action for a year …. He is in every way a self-made man, just as Bruce Wayne made himself into Batman. Bane made himself into Bane, but with much darker purposes.[31]

Dixon continued: "Bane is badassery personified. He's big and scary with a mind like a chess master. He's three steps ahead of whomever he's opposing at any time. Before the fight's begun he's set the rules and conditions that will lead to his victory. Your fate is decided long before you even know his name … you have a serious bad guy."[32] With this description in mind, one could have difficulties identifying this "serious bad guy" in the Schumacher variant of Bane portrayed in *Batman & Robin* with the wrestler Robert "Jeep" Swenson, who plays the character as a mostly silent and mindless henchman to Thurman's Poison Ivy. For years after the premiere of the 1997s blockbuster, fans have been going mad over this approach to one of the 1990s most significant archenemies in the Dark Knight's gallery as yet another "wrong understanding" or "misconception" of the source material. But maybe this idea for Bane's stultification is actually a consequence of Schumacher's challenging approach towards the 1990s topical uber-seriousness and gender tropes in comics that he clearly tried to overcome. With this "queering" aspect aimed towards Batman's most "serious" opponent in the 1990s comics, Jeep Swenson himself is giving here probably the best justification of this Bane-Poison Ivy flipped and gender-swapped hierarchy as "almost like the relationship between George and Lenny in *Of Mice and Men*, with the more diminutive person taking charge and telling the bigger one how to think" (Scivally 2011: 278).

In these circumstances, the decision to place prominent rubber nipples on Val Kilmer's and George Clooney's costumes in both Schumacher films amounts to an almost subversive act, manifesting yet another effort to breach Batman's strict formula demanding a depiction befitting the serious and brooding character. For Schumacher, the nipple move does not so much manifest any sexual fixation but strives to displace the hero beyond the dark tones, into much less obsessive and hermetic representation. Both his depictions of the Bruce Wayne/Batman persona are in fact counter-readings, since in *Batman Forever* Val Kilmer's Bruce Wayne is something of an insecure romantic looking for affection from his female companion, Dr. Chase Meridian ("'Val is sleek, pantherlike. He plays Batman in a more sensual way, whereas Michael, because he's not such a big guy, played him as very tough, aggressive'"[33]), while George Clooney's playboy in *Batman and Robin* is a vigilante no more, becoming a dad-like figure for Robin and Batgirl instead. The "visual queering" discernible in these works is an ongoing process as, in the director's approach, the "queer" aspect effectively serves as yet another tool to un-darken the Dark Knight by employing "subordinate" visual cues with a "dominant" superhero figure. Consequently, Schumacher exploits the aesthetic presence of Batman as an opportunity to contravene the traditional code of depicting the character, altering the standard motifs of an athletic "unsexualized" physicality by sudden and unexpected visual intrusion, such as the hysterical close-ups of buttocks and a crotch in both films. This "sexing up" of Batman's appearance as well as his increasingly diversified range of fancy, toyetic gadgets and vehicles leads to what Larrie Dudenhoeffer considers a symptomatic representation in Schumacher's first film:

> How do Batman and Robin realign the spatio-visual coordinates of the diegesis, and also remove the question mark that the Riddler traces over the Bat-signal to cast into doubt their intelligence, their masculine determination, and the cultural eminence of their "brand"? They inundate the screen with sexier tools, weapons, and vehicles, with Robin steering a sleeker Batboat to the shores of Claw Island and Batman flying a new Batwing across the waters, one that can transform into a submersible.
>
> (2017: 103)

The "nipple-ing" of Schumacher's Neon Knight goes much farther than merely breaking the visual standards of portrayal applicable to that hero. Besides a notable yet seemingly pointless effort to maintain a gender-accurate depiction, one could rightfully argue that this controversy has little to do with the essential realignment of the Dark Knight into the Camp Knight/Cute Knight/Dad Knight derivative. At this point, however, one needs to refer to the earlier Dad Knight, who appeared in the low-budget Filmation cartoons; Schumacher's visually non-dominant vigilante leaves the comfortable shadows both aesthetically and thematically, since Schumacher is bold enough to commit possibly the gravest offense towards the Dark Knight by posing another vital riddle: can Batman actually be happy? To underscore this dramatic turn in Batman's characterization one may consider another range of tie-in products—the official soundtracks to both Schumacher movies, whose promotional keynotes included two sentimental love ballads, i.e., Seal's *Kiss from a Rose* written for *Batman Forever* and *Gotham City* by R. Kelly for *Batman & Robin*. Although the films were accompanied by songs with more edge (U2's *Hold me, Thrill me, Kiss me, Kill me* and *The End is the Beginning is the End* by Smashing Pumpkins), those two tangibly sentimental tunes proved emblematic of the Schumacher-directed Batmen through meaningful lyrics, with a veiled allusion to sexual encounter in Seal's composition (inferred in the chorus: "Baby, I compare you to a kiss from a rose on the grey / Ooh, the more I get of you, stranger it feels, yeah / And now that your rose is in bloom / A light hits the gloom on the grey") and the clearly non-depressing image of the "traditionally" gloomy Gotham City (R. Kelly sings: "A city of justice, a city of love, a city of peace / For every one of us / We all need it, can't live without it / A Gotham City, oh yeah"). Both themes, written for a melancholic lover and an optimistic member of an urban community, are correspondingly interpreted onscreen by Val Kilmer and George Clooney under the guidance of Joel Schumacher.

Despite the arguments for treating the Burtonverse and the Schumacherverse as distinct in view of their tonal and aesthetic choices, it may be more productive to approach the latter as an expansion of the former, to which it added the artistic neon component as well as continuing to take the story of both Batman and Bruce Wayne into narrative territories where Burton's outcast would evolve into a much more balanced and socialized persona. If Burton wanted to see his protagonist as "this guy [who] wants to remain as hidden as possible and in the shadows as possible and unrevealing about himself"[34] in *Batman* and *Batman Returns*, *Batman Forever* and *Batman & Robin* forge a character who leaves the shadows and works through some of the issues that had made him an aloof loner in the first place. Again, one could ask whether this is the right way to portray Batman? What if, removed from his "natural" environment, he would lose his "essential" attributes? Here, the premise of necessary acceptance for the unorthodox re-envisioning of the Dark Knight comes into play again, a reprise which may yield unfamiliar yet still inspiring and refreshing incarnations of the character.

This is precisely the case with Schumacher's films, which may be disparaged for how their themes were ultimately executed, but it would be unfair to deny the director the right to look for his own "taste" of the character, even though it may be situated outside the "mandatory" domain of Batman's previous installments. Unquestionably, Joel Schumacher's Batman is the Batman who resonates with Joel Schumacher as an individual, especially considering what the screenwriters for *Batman Forever*—Janet and Lee Batchler—share:

> [Tim Burton] is a very gentle, erudite man. He's quiet, he seems a little shy ... he's full of enthusiasm and there's a childlike quality in the very best sense that comes out in all of his work .... Joel has that to a certain extent

too although he manifests himself differently. He's a New Yorker and just looking more like a cosmopolitan guy.[35]

Batchler's remark about his cosmopolitan input offers an interesting clue, implying a much more inclusive approach in working with the character and conceiving Batman as a less psychologically hermetic and more socialized individual. This is an essential element that links *Batman Forever* and *Batman & Robin*—an effort to envision both Batman and Bruce Wayne as living parts of their private and public ecosystems, a definite step forward in comparison to Burton's much more socially awkward persona. In *Batman Forever*, the post-Burton lone avenger finally develops a relationship with his partner in trade when Robin appears, which Schumacher conveys in two significant shots showing Robin reach for Batman's hand after the confrontation with Two-Face and the reversed gesture in Batman's climactic dive to save his companion in The Riddler's lair. In addition, there is the character's refreshing experience of genuine love involving Dr. Meridian (after all, Kilmer's Bruce confesses to Alfred in one scene: "I've never been in love before, Alfred"), as a further illustration of the slow progression in Batman's emotional make-up.

With the dominant trope in Schumacher's Batman films as the main hero's journey to abandon, figuratively speaking, his mental and emotional "batcave" and open himself up to other people (which one can see as the shift from Burton's shy impersonation to Schumacher's cosmopolitanism), it is a real shame that the final cut of *Batman Forever* didn't contain the highly meaningful scene commonly referred to today as the "Secret of the Batcave" or the "Man-Bat scene," which was actually shot and is widely available today through almost all the available DVD and Blu-ray editions of the film. This cut material comes from the third act of the movie and shows Bruce Wayne healing after the previous brutal raid by The Riddler and Two-Face in Wayne Manor and the Batcave that ends with the kidnapping of Chase Meridian and the devastation of Batman's lair. As Bruce is trying to regain his strength after being shot by Two-Face, he enters a hidden part of his hideout that appears to be the exact place that young Bruce had fallen years ago and decided to accept his vengeful mission. The fallen hero then finds here his father's journal—a red book that was mentioned earlier in the film as Thomas Wayne's private memoir, which ended with the tragic deaths of Dr. Wayne and his wife. In the official cut of the movie, the red book is simply an item that Bruce mentions during his conversation with Dr. Meridian in the still-progressing process of accepting the irreversible loss of his parents. The more elaborate scene that was eventually cut from the movie, however, gives a much more complex storyline as Wayne, just before heading to his final confrontation with The Riddler and Two-Face, gains here a chance to confront his inner demons and the fears that are destabilizing his personality throughout the film. Looking at the last entry written in the journal by his father, Bruce finds the following sentence: "Bruce insists on seeing a movie tonight … But Martha and I have our hearts set on Zorro, so Bruce's cartoon will have to wait until next week."

This simple yet quite revolutionary idea planted by the screenwriters of *Batman Forever* gives Batman a final resolution to all his guilt and broodiness following Wayne's incorrect assumption that he was responsible for his parents' tragic fate. Moreover, by finally facing Bruce Wayne's past and rediscovering the actual origin of his Batman persona, Schumacher is letting Batman leave his grim personality and guilt-driven understanding of his mission so dominant in the traditional Dark Knight's depictions. Visually, this moment of heading into a new understanding of his finally balanced character is portrayed here by an astounding encounter between Wayne and a giant man-sized bat creature emerging majestically from the cave's darkness. In just one brief yet iconic moment, Bruce and the bat face each other, with both figures spreading out their arms/wings in an act of almost perfect reflection. This "communion" between Man and Bat is probably the most significant, but paradoxically not existing in the final theatrical footage, the moment of the Schumacher-helmed cinematic curatorship over Batman as the Dark Knight is finally able to leave here his "Dark" attitude of being a vengeful crusader for a much more affirmative and optimistic idea of actually enjoying being Batman. With Wayne leaving the cave after this revelation with a smile on his face, it's not hard to interpret this whole sequence as a breakthrough in the entire Batman cinematic franchise mythology as the hero realizes that he should not be seen anymore as an effect of his inner rage but rather his inner need to bring hope and justice. Hence this deleted material actually completes one minor yet significant hint from the earlier part of the movie when Wayne visits Doctor Chase Meridian's office for the first time and asks about the inkblot image hanging on the wall: "You have a thing for bats?". In response he hears: "Oh, that's a Rorschach, Mr. Wayne. An ink blot. People see what they want. I think the question would be do you have a thing for bats?". The answer is: yes, Bruce Wayne is Batman not because of his guilt or some bat-related trauma but because he truly likes the role and imagery of the bat-shaped hero. Batman's responsibilities are not a burden after all, instead serving as the compatible component of Bruce Wayne's private life, with both sides to be celebrated and not suffocated.

The shift from his original introversion goes even further in *Batman & Robin*, whose subplot culminates in the first ever cinematic Bat-family, not to mention the truly personal and heart-warming interactions between Clooney's Batman and Michael Gough's fatherly Alfred during the latter's terminal illness. Both topics are referred to in the 1997 main narrative, in two significant conversations between Bruce and Alfred concerning Batman's need to control everything and everyone around him (as Alfred explains Robin/Dick Grayson's stubborn attitude: "Despite all your talents, you are still a novice in the ways of family. Master Dick follows the same star as you but gets there by his own course. You must learn to trust him, for that is the nature of family"). Finally, the butler advances what is possibly the best diagnosis of the Caped Crusader's core idealistic motivation, rooted profoundly in the loss of his loved ones: "Death and chance stole your parents. But rather than become a victim, you have done everything in your power to control the fates. For what is Batman? If not an effort to master the chaos that sweeps our world, an attempt to control death itself."

The two essential themes in Schumacher's Batmen could be summarized as follows: in *Batman Forever* a major storyline illustrates how the protagonist seeks some sort of balance in sustaining his dual identity, as Batman begins to predominate over the non-heroic alter ego, whereas in *Batman & Robin* the un-Darkened Knight is finally shown as an individual who had already transcended his traumatic motivation and pursues his vigilante quest not out of revenge but rather as a consciously assumed duty to ensure Gotham City's well-being. All four movies directed by Tim Burton and Joel Schumacher reveal a story arc in which Batman in 1989 is initially a figure taken nearly straight out of a horror story, who then demonstrates greater openness towards the equally mentally disturbed Selina Kyle/Catwoman in 1992, faces his unresolved character dichotomy in 1995 and then confronts The Riddler and Two-Face, whose respective goals are to destroy the superhero and the playboy personas. Ultimately, it focuses on Bruce Wayne/Batman as a bone fide protector of his newly founded Bat-family in 1997, while the subplot of Alfred's imminent passing marks Bruce's symbolical transition from someone who needs wise assistance to someone who realizes that now his young protégés require his support and mentoring. Schumacher's concluding notion concerning Wayne and Batman is epitomized in the final scenes in both movies: in *Batman Forever*, Val Kilmer's protagonist spectacularly saves both his love interest Dr. Chase Meridian and his newly found partner Robin during The Riddler's sadistic game of choice, crowned with the iconic: "I had to save them both, I'm both Bruce Wayne and Batman. Not because I have to be, now because I choose to be." In the final scene of *Batman & Robin*, George Clooney's Batman stands over the defeated Mr. Freeze and delivers a speech that may be construed as an implicit commentary on the whole Batman quadrilogy and the slow recovery of the Dark Knight from the vengeful and brutal Noir-tmare Knight towards a family-oriented iteration in Schumacher's Neon Knight: "Vengeance isn't power. Anyone can take a life. But to give life … that's true power." This particular Batman finally enjoys being Batman, leaves his childhood trauma behind as well as moves out of the reclusive Batcave: an image that very aptly reflects Schumacher's feat of trespassing on the only territory that Batman fans definitely consider a forbidden no man's land—the realm of the bright Dad Knight. Regarding the final reinterpretation of Batman delivered by George Clooney, Schumacher recalled:

> I felt since we were going to make another one that we needed to be progressive. I wanted to get away and the reason I chose George is I very much wanted to get away from the dark, brooding, self-obsessed narcissistic Batman … and give the audience, especially the young audience, a Batman who is more enlightened, who perhaps thinks of others first.[36]

This idea could evolve even further if the eventually scrapped plans for the next of Schumacher's Batman projects after *Batman & Robin* materialize. As Gary Collinson reports, even before the premiere of Schumacher's second installment in the franchise, the Warner Bros. studio was interested in giving the director a chance to helm yet another sequel which was discussed quite deeply by Batman's fandom (see Collinson 2012: 120) over recent years. According to Collinson and numerous other reports, the main screenwriter for *Batman 5*, scheduled for release in summer 1999, was Mark Protosevich, whose initial script was commonly referred to as *Batman Unchained*, although a competing title, *Batman Triumphant*, had also emerged as a result of fan-made screenplays floating over the internet and trying to follow Protosevich's hints about his draft. What transpires from some existing, exciting clues about this eventually-abandoned project is actually a fascinating idea for Schumacher's third take on Batman, being at the same time almost an *Avengers: Endgame*-type of an assemble movie trying to sum up the whole of the Batman cinematic franchise of 1989–97. As in the previous Schumacher blockbusters, *Batman Unchained* was supposed to include yet another pair of main villains, with Scarecrow and Harley Quinn as the leading antagonists. With some rumored casting choices for both rogues, an interesting list of names such as Nicolas Cage, Steve Buscemi, Robert Englund, Jeff Goldblum, Ewan McGregor, and even the popular rapper Coolio appears as possible candidates for the role of the lunatic, fear-obsessed scientist Dr. Jonathan Crane vel Scarecrow. Courtney Love and Madonna were also rumored to be Schumacher's top choices for Harley Quinn—a creation from Paul Dini and Bruce Timm introduced in the "Joker's Favor" episode of *Batman: The Animated Series* in September 1992 as Joker's henchwoman, reimagined for the Schumacher's version as Joker's daughter. Some other minor casting predictions, like Martin Short's idea for the secondary role of a Mad Hatter villain, were also circulating, suggesting a possible new character build-up for the expansion of a new "wave" of Batman films after *Batman Unchained/Triumphant* with a new set of villains that would continue the Burton/Schumacher line in the eventually never-to-happen future.

What is interesting about this finally scrapped project of 1999s *Batman 5*, however, is its actual place in the continuity of a Schumacher-helmed franchise, serving as yet another attempt from the director to resolve one of the most troubling legacies of the 1990s Batman films—namely, Batman's willingness to take the lives of his enemies (like the Joker or Penguin in Burton movies and Two-Face in *Batman Forever*). By looking at some minor details about the Protosevich take, there appears a plot that would combine Harley Quinn's efforts to avenge her father's death in the 1989 movie with Scarecrow's deadly fear toxin that was meant to make Batman have nightmarish visions of all the villains that he consciously or randomly killed throughout the franchise (with respective cameos from actors like Jack Nicholson and Danny de Vito to be expected). Although it is quite difficult to discuss a project that was never fully developed, these few ideas provide a thrilling taste of Schumacher's final installment to his trilogy, seemingly still following his willingness to exorcise Batman's darker tropes and previous sins during his confrontation with a complete gallery of his onscreen villains. As Protosevich admitted recently: "Joel wanted to tie up all of the films. The Tim Burton films and his films, building up to this moment."[37] The "unchained" or "triumphant" aspect of Batman as signaled in these semi-official or strictly fan-generated titles could eventually mean the definitive closure of Schumacher's take on the main character, letting Batman rise beyond his quite often deadly depictions and narrative chains of being a death-bringer to his enemies in the earlier movies and to triumph as the much more positive hero which Schumacher was heading towards in his two previous productions. Although it is a shame that this plan never came to existence, it is not hard to imagine that if eventually made, *Batman Unchained* wouldn't be—as some may expect—a drastic change of tone for Schumacher's Neon Knight but rather a conscious succession of 1997s *Batman & Robin* with all the potentially expected signs of Schumacher's characterization of Batman as well as his visual depictions.

Thus, it all boils down to one critical factor—the execution. As promising as the balance-searching story in *Batman Forever* may appear and as provocatively compelling as the "happy Batman" concept may sound, it would be legitimate to say that both themes feature only perfunctorily in Schumacher's films. After all, major parts of the original screenplay were removed from the theatrical cut of the first feature while the overwhelmingly ecstatic and comedic aspect of the subsequent movie downplays the more serious elements such as Alfred's sickness and possible death. However, even with these obvious shortcomings both of Schumacher's contributions to the Batman franchise are undoubtedly distinctive, introducing novel and/or unexpected elements to the overall Batman oeuvre. Given the final shape, one could recall Schumacher's own idealistic appraisal shared at the 2012 Camerimage Festival, where he chaired the jury: "Nothing's better or worse. Is just different."[38]

It does sound like something a director would say to justify themselves in the eyes of the disappointed audiences, but with Schumacher it is rather another manifestation of his inclusive approach to filmmaking and storytelling, one that challenges the artistic status quo to make use of new and non-canonical forms and stories. The three areas discussed above—the film-related toys, games, and the final "nipple bias" of Schumacher's take on Batman—are conceivably the constitutive elements of the Lite Knight, which derive from the Neon Knight's overall structure. Judging by the strategies adopted in toy manufacturing, game development, and onscreen character building, the trespassive ingredient in Schumacher's artistic approach certainly describes the direction he took with Batman in that it avoids all conventional elements and forms of exploitation. The Neon Knight's lite-ness contests keeping Batman within narrow dark corridors—onscreen and offscreen—and demands a broadening of the character's presence and capabilities in plastic form, virtual simulation, and diegetic interpretation alike. Schumacher's Neon Knight embodied by Val Kilmer and George Clooney is a distantly removed cousin of his most iconic protagonist, i.e., *Tigerland*'s Bozz, as both of these characters openly reject the emotionally hermetic and very masculine attributes of the "proper" screen and wartime heroes. The forever-ness of Batman—in all likelihood the most serious concern associated with Schumacher's approach—is thus vindicated through his weird notion of more than one Batman: a truly "floating" concept that can accommodate even manifestly un-Batman-like attributes. On the other hand, this may be indicative of the main "problem" with his films, since "Schumacher's Batman is fundamentally a different kind of man, a grown-up who moved past the limitations of revenge as a singular motivation and into a more holistic understanding of justice. This Batman had it both ways, too—he got to be emotionally available and got to look fabulous while doing it."[39] Still, the good thing is that, albeit initially underestimated, the radically "different" Batman eventually managed to garner significant praise for his conceptual otherness. Regrettably, the most substantial acclaim it received coincided with the death of Joel Schumacher on June 22, 2020.

Notes

1   Dominic Wells, "'Woody Allen Changed My Life': Joel Schumacher Q&A," Londonhollywood.wordpress.com, November 3, 2014, https://londonhollywood.wordpress.com/2014/11/03/woody-allen-changed-my-life-joel-schumacher-qa/.

2   Owen Gleiberman, "Remembering Joel Schumacher: A Stylish Director Who Was Always Willing to Take Chances," Variety.com, June 22, 2020, https://variety.com/2020/film/columns/joel-schumacher-dead-tribute-batman-forever-falling-down-1234645492/amp/.
3   Andrew Goldman, "In Conversation: Joel Schumacher," Vulture.com, June 22, 2020, https://www.vulture.com/2020/06/joel-schumacher-in-conversation.html.
4   Matthew Hays, "Joel Schumacher: Reluctant and Conflicted Gay Trailblazer," Advocate.com, June 24, 2020, https://www.advocate.com/commentary/2020/6/24/joel-schumacher-reluctant-and-conflicted-gay-trailblazer?amp.
5   Tegan O'Neil, "The Light that you Shine Can Be Seen," tcj.com, June 30, 2021, https://www.tcj.com/the-light-that-you-shine-can-be-seen/.
6   Manufacturing Intellect, "Joel Schumacher Interview (2000)," YouTube, 2017, https://www.youtube.com/watch?v=bn8H75Tv8q0&t=400s.
7   Warner Bros. Entertainment, "Batman / Behind the scenes of Batman Forever and Batman & Robin / Warner Bros. Entertainment," YouTube, 2021, https://www.youtube.com/watch?v=AB9tlLKPZJ0&list=PLvOhZIQVv6hBvq8nIHmaVMfZP0ya5a0i7&index=69.
8   Jason Bailey, "Don't Forget that Joel Schumacher Briefly Saved Batman," nytimes.com, June 23, 2020, https://www.nytimes.com/2020/06/23/movies/joel-schumacher-batman.html.
9   Manufacturing Intellect, "Joel Schumacher Interview on 'Batman Forever' (1995)," YouTube, 2017, https://www.youtube.com/watch?v=cNX_ZIr33tI&t=433s.
10 Ibid.
11 Daniel Dockery, "Batman Returns is the Most Anti-Franchise Franchise Movie Ever Made," Polygon.com, June 14, 2022, https://www.polygon.com/23165989/batman-returns-30th-anniversary-tim-burton.
12 Warner Bros. Entertainment, "Batman Returns / Shadows of the Bat: Dark Side of the Knight / Warner Bros. Entertainment," YouTube, 2021, https://www.youtube.com/watch?v=JKMSKvJncf4&list=PLvOhZIQVv6hBvq8nIHmaVMfZP0ya5a0i7&index=26.
13 Ibid.
14 LilCosgrove, "A Closer Look: Batman Returns' Impact on Children (July 1992)," YouTube, 2018, https://www.youtube.com/watch?v=KWxrHz-JORE&list=PLvOhZIQVv6hBvq8nIHmaVMfZP0ya5a0i7&index=36.
15 Collier Jennings, "How the Batman Returns McDonald's Ad Campaign Changed the Series," Slashfilm.com, February 11, 2022, https://www.slashfilm.

com/764908/how-the-batman-returns-mcdonalds-ad-campaign-changed-the-series/?fbclid=IwAR0mz8jFHABRAvORB3MjVgvz1olme3eBQ91FKC6pTDR34-UBLGM6ck3ehFQ.

16 Math Erao, "Batman's Michael Keaton on Clashing with Schumacher over 'Dark' Bruce Wayne," CBR.com, January 3, 2022, https://www.cbr.com/batman-michael-keaton-bruce-wayne-joel-schumacher-vision/?fbclid=IwAR1OwSeG11ZS5SuhSV4cCUDNR0jiKulZtSbXsXepLanbfpr2PFe9Y0-Jch0.

17 Ben Aldis, "Why Schumacher's Batman Movies Aren't Set in Burton's Universe," Screenrant.com, April 12, 2020, https://screenrant.com/batman-schumacher-movie-not-burton-universe-explained/?fbclid=IwAR3T6zGMm9LmXsccm7Q00RR84z2b8nLcxAV3L2Hld1QT15dhdSVP1hn9YjA.

18 Flashback FilmMaking, "The Making of 'Batman Forever': Behind the Scenes," YouTube, 2019, https://www.youtube.com/watch?v=oQu00cQzRnk&list=PL356E849FE3566CFF&index=10.

19 Ibid.

20 Ibid.

21 Warner Bros. Entertainment, "Batman / Behind the Scenes of Batman Forever and Batman & Robin / Warner Bros. Entertainment," YouTube, 2021, https://www.youtube.com/watch?v=AB9tlLKPZJ0&list=PLvOhZIQVv6hBvq8nIHmaVMfZP0ya5a0i7&index=69.

22 Ibid.

23 Ibid.

24 Trevor McDonald's Midnight Rodeo, "Why is Batman Forever? The Making of Batman Forever 1995," YouTube, 2021, https://www.youtube.com/watch?v=Kb-BSZIoprI&list=PLvOhZIQVv6hBvq8nIHmaVMfZP0ya5a0i7&index=55&ab_channel=CultCollectibleMerchandise.

25 Tegan O'Neil, "The Light that you Shine Can Be Seen," tcj.com, June 30, 2021, https://www.tcj.com/the-light-that-you-shine-can-be-seen/.

26 Andrew P. Alderete, "The Music of 'Batman Forever' by Elliott Goldenthal," YouTube, 2011, https://www.youtube.com/watch?v=A-SUl6_-aEc&list=PLvOhZIQVv6hBvq8nIHmaVMfZP0ya5a0i7&index=46.

27 John C. Tibbetts Interviews, "Joel Schumacher Interview for Batman Forever (1995)," YouTube, 2022, https://www.youtube.com/watch?v=pUDO97HeEBE.

28 Superhero Stuff You Should Know, "The History of Batman Kenner Action Figures – Part 2 (Batman Forever, Batman & Robin, Batman Beyond)," YouTube,

2022, https://www.youtube.com/watch?v=cGwyq99ucWA&list=PLvOhZIQVv6hBvq8nIHmaVMfZP0ya5a0i7&index=89&ab_channel=SuperheroStuffYouShouldKnow.

29 Movies To Video Games Reviews, "Movies to Video Games Review – Batman Forever (SNES, GEN, DOS)," YouTube, 2018, https://www.youtube.com/watch?v=txvACJATlD0&ab_channel=MoviesToVideoGamesReviews.

30 Blair Farrell, "Review: Batman Forever: The Arcade Game (PSONE)," comicbookvideogames.com, June 16, 2015, https://comicbookvideogames.com/2015/06/16/review-batman-forever-the-arcade-game-psone/.

31 Chris Begley, "Who Is Bane? His Creator Discusses the Character," batman-news.com, January 27, 2011, https://batman-news.com/2011/01/27/who-is-bane-his-creator-discusses-the-character/.

32 Todd Matthy, "An Interview with Bane Creator Chuck Dixon," toddmatthy.com, August 15, 2012, https://toddmatthy.com/2012/08/15/an-interview-with-bane-creator-chuck-dixon/.

33 Richard Natale, "'Batman' Paints the Town: The Caped Crusaders Are Hipper, Sleeker and Suited Up with Sex Appeal. A Colorful Comic-Book Look Replaces Gotham's Dark Past," latimes.com, June 13, 1995, https://www.latimes.com/archives/la-xpm-1995-06-13-ca-12546-story.html.

34 Warner Bros. Entertainment, "Batman Returns / Shadows of the Bat: Dark Side of the Knight / Warner Bros. Entertainment," YouTube, 2021, https://www.youtube.com/watch?v=JKMSKvJncf4&list=PLvOhZIQVv6hBvq8nIHmaVMfZP0ya5a0i7&index=26.

35 Superhero Stuff You Should Know, "The Truth about Burton's Batman 3 – Batman Forever Screenwriters' Interview – Janet and Lee Batchler," YouTube, 2020, https://www.youtube.com/watch?v=IzHBWv1t30I&list=PLvOhZIQVv6hBvq8nIHmaVMfZP0ya5a0i7&index=3.

36 The Bobby Wygant Archive, "Joel Schumacher 'Batman And Robin' 1997 – Bobbie Wygant Archive," YouTube, 2022, https://www.youtube.com/watch?v=2lBFLPt-JVo&list=PLvOhZIQVv6hBvq8nIHmaVMfZP0ya5a0i7&index=51.

37 Rob Leane, "Batman Triumphant: Examining the Sequel that Never Happened," denofgeek.com, March 21, 2016, https://www.denofgeek.com/movies/batman-triumphant-examining-the-sequel-that-never-happened/?fbclid=IwAR32b8pPkyns1c4WMPR1tFffSxca9rUz3tlXvHgkMyozQ-we1D05esgDd3o.

38 Camerimage Festival, "Camerimage Joel Schumacher Interview," YouTube, 2014, https://www.youtube.com/watch?v=ascSrBIbqNY.
39 Tegan O'Neil, "The Light that you Shine Can Be Seen," tcj.com, June 30, 2021, https://www.tcj.com/the-light-that-you-shine-can-be-seen/.

3

The Neon Knight triumphant: Modern perceptions of Joel Schumacher's Batman duology

3.1 "It's so bad, it's almost good": Fandom's online discourse after Joel Schumacher's passing

When on June 22, 2020 Joel Schumacher passed away from undisclosed cancer at the age of eighty, social media as well as various journals and magazines dedicated to arts and popular culture witnessed quite a deluge of appreciation posts as well as reminiscences from professional critics. What they shared was a rather unexpected number of fond memories and more objective insights into Schumacher's legacy, whose return to favor should be attributed to his unconventional approach, referred to in previous chapters. The analyses across news sites and entertainment periodicals on Schumacher drew readers' attention with titles such as "Joel Schumacher and the Non-Crisis of Infinite Batmans" (Wired.com), which followed up with: "*Batman Forever* and *Batman & Robin* have been punch lines since the '90s. But the director's death reminds us that everyone has their own Dark Knight." Other websites, for instance CBR.com and Batman-online.com, asserted in their tributes that "Batman Forever Is STILL the Dark Knight's Most Underrated movie"[1] or asked "Why Batman and Robin is the Underrated Gem of the Batman Franchise?"[2] This radical change in tone among the critics and fans discussing Schumacher's Batman films from nearly thirty years ago brought to mind a similar shift with respect to another "inappropriate" Batman text. After all, the 1966–98 *Batman* television show saw similar reinterpretation in which its original shortcomings became the most cherished elements in an act of nostalgic revival among the fans.

In a study on the re-emergence of the 1960s *Batman* as a valuable and esteemed iteration of the character, Lynn Spigel and Henry Jenkins suggested taking a detailed look into how fans in the 1990s perceived the campy entertainment starring Adam West, since they found it to be a sphere in which popular memory around the classic television series was constituted. This particular application of the notion of popular memory is crucial to Spigel and Jenkins's examination of how thirty- and forty-year-old viewers recalled a 1960s show from their childhood. Specifically, they construed it as a nostalgic phenomenon which combined individual memories of the viewing experience, whereby all the controversy which may have surrounded it was eliminated or ignored, so as to appreciate the role of the text in nurturing one's attachment to Batman as a fictional character. The authors employ Ulric Neisser's category of repisodic memory, which describes the actual mode of "remembering" cult objects as strongly subjectified incidents involving a strong tendency to dismiss the potentially unwanted actual details of a given cultural artifact. According to Spigel and Jenkins, "Popular memory thus tends to be prototypical and constructive, rather that specific and fixed. Even when interview participants talked about the programme, their accounts tended to be highly generic. Rather than remembering specific episodes, they remembered *Batman* in repisodic ways, expressing fondness for isolated but recurring images" (2015: 187).

As a result, Sigel and Jenkins observed highly interesting re-evaluations among adult fans of Batman, who looked back at their childhood fascination with substantially greater approval than one could have expected in view of the "dominant" media presence of Tim Burton's much darker Dark Knight in the last decade of twentieth century. Still, the Batman embodied by Adam West was indeed personally cherished, having been involved in most people's initial exposure to the character. Sigel and Jenkins continue: "Popular memories of *Batman* actively reworked the terms of its original reception, often appealing to a similar logic of nostalgia and cultural custodianship .... Our responders shared few of the original critics' anxiety about the programme's aesthetic status. ... So enmeshed had *Batman* become in their personal life histories that they did not feel compelled or even able to judge its merits' (2015: 185). The nature of the reception of the 1960s Batman after a considerable lapse of time perfectly illustrates the impact of the nostalgic factor on the formation of individual memory about a given phenomenon. Svetlana Boym observed: "Nostalgia is about the relationship between individual biography and the biography of groups or nations, between personal and collective memory" (2001: xvi), which quite accurately describes how thirty- and forty-year-old Bat-fans remembered earlier Batman manifestations and amalgamated their initial experience with 1990s features or animated shows like the acclaimed *Batman: The Animated Series*. Today, it may be possible to rewrite Sigel and Jenkins's work in relation to another originally "disregarded" Batman productions, which to numerous enthusiasts of the character have acquired considerable appeal. The fact that nostalgia-inducing texts in the shape of Schumacher's films increasingly receive positive attention offers valid grounds to examine how Batman manifests in the official and non-official discourse.

The official shift in the evaluations of Joel Schumacher's work with the Batman mythology is readily observed in the aforementioned press releases from 2020. The overall impression is that they predominantly discuss *Batman Forever* and *Batman & Robin* as original rather than disastrous and damaging envisionings of the character, which was certainly a common vibe in the majority of commentaries in the 1990s. Below are just a few such critical statements, as recalled by Will Brooker from the Zak Weisfeld's review of *Batman & Robin*:

> … whatever one's feelings for Tim Burton's first two gothic tales of Batman, they were at least consistent. There was a vision behind them — brooding, gloomy, sexy — a nerdy fantasy of transformation, through rubber suit, from dud to superhero. If there's a vision behind *Batman & Robin*, it is of big stacks of money. The sets, like the movie, are an overwhelming mess. Impressive at first, by virtue of size and number alone, one is quickly numbed by them, beaten into sensory submission by the busyness and clash of styles. … Burton used the Batman myth as a framework to hang one of his typically wan, existential "outsider" fashion shows. Schumacher has turned his two passes through Gotham into incomprehensible swirls of mayhem and art direction. … It's only as an exercise in set design that *Batman & Robin* succeeds, though it's all so over the top that it's more of an exercise in what not to do than anything else. Schumacher has chosen to

light his film with outlandishly garish neons and brilliant blues and pinks, which unfortunately make this look more like some ridiculous Batman on Ice escapade than anything else.

(Brooker 2000: 298–9)

The evident paradigm was to reject all Schumacher-specific traits: the "clash of styles," "outlandishly garish neons," or "ridiculous Batman," the indisputably "wrong" elements of that Dark Knight interpretation, followed by a reference to the much more "accurate" depiction in the vein of "brooding, gloomy, sexy" that this kind of story ostensibly called for. To be fair, a number of the more recent publications concerned with superhero cinema still find fault with Schumacher's work, as his movies continue to be widely and readily considered as instances of the "wrong" filmmaking in that genre. For instance, in *A Brief History of Comic Book Movies* (2017), Wheeler Winston Dixon and Richard Graham find *Batman & Robin* to be "desperately on the edge of straight out parody" (2017: 11), while Liam Burke's *The Pocket Essential Superhero Movies* from 2008 passes the following verdict: "Public enemy number one would have to be Joel Schumacher who, following on from *Batman Forever*'s mystifying box-office popularity, turned in an over-produced neon nightmare loosely resembling something a dog might throw up after ingesting too many glow-sticks and tinsel" (2008: 145). In *Superheroes! Capes and Crusaders in Comics and Films* (2008) Roz Kaveney notes that "Schumacher is certainly a significant part of the problem, here as in *Batman Forever*. He made the decision to opt for a light touch, in the name of making the franchise more 'family friendly', but his idea of a light touch is ill-timed and often tasteless jokes" (2008: 246). The dislike of Schumacher's Batmen consistently invokes the same assortment of allegations—"too bright" and "too silly"—while more pertinent remarks on deficient technical execution are mixed with general misgivings about the necessity of forcing Batman into the "neon nightmare" aesthetic. However, the tone shifted radically in post-2020 reflection, as critics and fans alike re-evaluated the reasoning behind the glow sticks embellishing the Dark Knight's appearance.

The outraged voices of the professional film critics were reinforced by the growing legions of displeased fans, who just when *Batman & Robin* premiere finally received a powerful tool of websites and online forums to manifest their deep concerns about the Neon Knight. Since all major grievances of the most committed fan critics were cited in the works of scholars such as Will Brooker or Glen Weldon, it will suffice to quote just one symptomatic vituperation from a forum debate entitled "Bring Me the Head of Joel Schumacher," which encapsulates the fierce resistance provoked by Schumacher's radical revision of the Batman franchise:

> Schumaker you little piss ant! Who the fuck gave you the right to direct anything remotely as cool as Batman? I'm a film major in my freshman year, and I can tell you right now I can direct a better film on crack with my mouth stitched closed and my eyeballs plucked out! I don't know what the fuck you were thinking … pick up a Batman comic book you asinine fool? Does Gotham City look like Club Expo to you? Do you see any neon? What the fuck? And NIPPLES? This isn't a fucking joke! Batman isn't some two-bit circus freak like your bearded lady of a mother! He is the essence of gothic darkness, a man ripped between reality and fantasy, teetering on the brink of insanity with only his partner and butler and his mission to keep him from going crazy! Did you capture any of these elements? Of course not, because obviously you must have gone to Ronald McDonald School of Film? Who's the next villain, Schumacher, you schmuck, you prick … the Hamburglar? FLICK YOU!
>
> (Brooker 2000: 306)

This emotional response to Schumacher's vision essentially lists all the elements that have been shown in this book as the most "personal" and potentially valuable contributions of the director. As this particular forum user explicitly yet accurately articulates it in this somewhat unsophisticated criticism, the main concern is the EXPO-like vision of the neon Gotham, the un-darkened appearance of the main vigilante, stripped of the brooding qualities, and the commercial context of both of Schumacher's features, proud representatives of the Ronald McDonald School of Film. In short, the very elements that actually launched the Neon Knight as conceived by Joel Schumacher were treated with the same disdain by film critics and regular viewers alike—the process of neon-izing Batman and his environment, as well as the framework of the neon-lit storytelling, were clearly perceived as objectionable and pointless messing about with the essence of such elements, leading to the inevitable eradication of the compelling and "serious" qualities in Batman cinematic lore. Such a notion is still strongly apparent in the many retrospections on Schumacher's legacy, but importantly significant departures from that excessively negative discourse can be observed; the appreciative commentaries became even more prominent following the director's passing.

To elucidate this new approach towards the previously unappreciated elements of Schumacher's duology, one should delve—with due caution—into the abundant domain of semi-professional or strictly fandom news sites and webpages—commonly edited by fans-turned online journalists, scoopers, and newscasters. Interestingly, more insightful observations mingle there with an inclination typical of the milieu, namely to hype up the content and opt for less analytical and more emotional approaches to a given topic. In fact, such news sites perfectly demonstrate how popular memory is shaped among the most involved readers and followers of popular culture. Schumacher's problematic Batman films and their recognition in this particular type of modern online criticism clearly displays the aforementioned pattern of developing nostalgic notions relating to a given phenomenon, conceptions negotiated between historical concerns of the earlier critical response and the repisodic memory of today's editors and readers, in which *Batman Forever* and *Batman & Robin* appear to possess significant nostalgic potential. The hindsight perspective on Schumacher's works—notably those published after the director's passing—may reveal how problematic elements in the movies actually inspire new interpretations, marked by considerable approval for the Neon Knight idea.

In the majority of the appreciative comments and articles online, the common motif is highlighting the "otherness" of Schumacher's approach to the Batman franchise. One of the most representative among many of those is John Shin's commentary published on June 24, 2020 on CBR.com entitled "Batman Forever Is STILL the Dark Knight's Most Underrated Movie." The authors principle assertion is as follows:

> With director Joel Schumacher's passing, it may be time for a reevaluation of his much-maligned *Batman Forever*. … The result was a campy, visually sumptuous take on the characters, with thrilling action sequences and

standout performances from Jim Carrey as the Riddler and Tommy Lee Jones as Two-Face.... Visually, it is one of the most stunning Batman movies. Some have criticized the movie's dialogue, but given its campy nature, it is fitting. Along with this, the excellent performances from Carrey and Jones pick up any slack. Though it has earned a bad reputation compared to other Batman films, the movie has enough strong points that it's worth a reappraisal.[3]

Shin underlines that the greatest asset of Schumacher's feature is its "stunning" quality, achieved through the overall design of the diegetic world as well as superior acting, which the author clearly considers to be integral parts of the Schumacher-orchestrated environment. Once denigrated as "lunatic," the onscreen behavior of the heroes and villains is another component that the commentators often appreciate for its "goofiness" instead of rejecting it for its over-the-top theatricality. The two main antagonists of Schumacher's movies—Jim Carrey's sneaky The Riddler from 1995 and Uma Thurman's seductive Poison Ivy from 1997—seem to gain increasing appreciation now, as the editor of the online entertainment news website Collider, Brecken Hunter Wellborn, observes:

> There may be other campy supervillains, but there are none who embody the joys of camp as fully as Poison Ivy. Ivy's camp pleasures reside in her self-aware performance of femininity, which suggests that gender itself is just a performance. Through her exaggerated, spectacularized enactment of hyper-femininity, Ivy makes a farce of gender. Twenty-five years since *Batman & Robin*'s release, Poison Ivy remains the definitive camp supervillain icon.[4]

A similar reassessment of Carrey's The Riddler is made by John Holmes from Movieweb:

> If we were to cull Jim Carrey's overacting as The Riddler from *Batman Forever*'s world (a place already burdened with bad dialogue and overall ridiculous performances) then there would be much less warranted gold for us to look back on the film altogether. Jim Carrey's take on The Riddler isn't disappointing, not at all, but rather a product of something much larger. A garish cog in a very loud clock. His input is, in every sense of the word, chaotic — and a movie as chaotic and high energy as *Batman Forever* required that.[5]

Even Val Kilmer's portrayal of Bruce Wayne in *Batman Forever*—once universally denounced as bland and uninspired—draws more interest now, with, for instance, Christian Colby Eltell reconsidering his performance in the tellingly titled "Batman Forever is Actually a Better Batman Movie than People Remember": "*Batman Forever* may be remembered mostly for its over-the-top comic book storyline, but Val Kilmer's Batman/Bruce Wayne is also memorable for dis-playing the character's internal struggles. The chemistry between him and Chase is also slightly more open and effective than the relationships in Burton's films, especially in terms of understanding his dual identity."[6]

Recent commentaries on Schumacher's Batman legacy constitute truly intriguing material, because almost every flaw noted in 1995 and 1997 is nowadays rehashed into an actual advantage in those productions over later incarnations of the hero in cinema. In fact, a separate section in this chapter would be required to cover the renewed appreciation for *Batman & Robin*, which recognizes that the film's bizarre form and tonal silliness are entertaining rather than embarrassing. For example, Rosie Knight from Nerdist openly admits in "Why Batman and Robin is the Underrated Gem of the Batman Franchise" that

> *Batman and Robin* is in fact a celebration of everything great about the wacky origins of the Caped Crusader. Though it's in no way perfect, it's actually a wonderfully fun exploration of Bat-lore and a love-filled homage to the colorful capers of Batman'66. ... Nothing's too ridiculous for Schumacher and screenwriter Akiva Goldsman's Gotham, and there's such reckless joy to be found in that. A truly fun vision of Batman's world where heroes can surf through the atmosphere and villains can kill you with a kiss after making you fight your best bud for the right to receive that deadly smooch–what's not to love about *Batman & Robin*?[7]

It is particularly interesting that the fans and critics concur as to the very nature of *Batman & Robin*. While *Batman Forever* maintains a more serious story, many reviewers happen to actually enjoy the wackiness of Schumacher's second feature since "perfection isn't necessary. Thankfully, recent years have been kinder to this film. Since the franchise got back-on-track, most people look back at *Batman & Robin* and laugh. And why shouldn't we? Most of it was intended to be funny. That's right. You didn't think Arnold's ice puns were meant to be serious, did you?"[8] A similar sentiment is expressed by the author of Martin's Movie Review, whose comment about the 1997 film also offers a very relevant observation regarding its "welcoming" or non-exclusive aspect:

> I'm not saying that *B&R* is great. It's far from that, but it's NOT horrible, it's actually the perfect introduction to the world of Gotham City for children under the age of ten. That's a huge demographic the last time I checked. Why can't it be respected on that level? ... The whole idea of one particular group of people claiming ownership over Batman is absurd anyway. The character doesn't belong to anybody. There's dozens of different versions and interpretations on page and screen spanning over seventy-five years, which means everyone in the world has THEIR Batman.[9]

In short, this realigned approach recognizes Schumacher's innovative style and execution, while its outcomes are acknowledged as a legitimate variant of superhero-centric cinematic production. Perhaps the most impressive and unexpected upshot of the revived discourse surrounding Schumacher after 2020 is that one now discerns and values the much more inclusive—both aesthetically and thematically—vision of the Neon Knight, which used to be universally spurned. Today, this aspect is given sincere praise throughout mainstream geek culture websites and in the online activities and statements of film aficionados. Paradoxically enough, the recent debate concerning Schumacher's duology in the geek and nerd milieu—which highlights the fun and entertaining quality—was perhaps best recapitulated by Val Kilmer himself, as recounted by David Crew in a Den of Geek post:

> In one telling anecdote, he recalled agreeing to show the movie to his children a few years after its release, but he had to drive into town from his New Mexico ranch to buy it because he didn't own a VHS copy in his home. After the film started, his children quietly shuffled out one-by-one within the first 20 minutes, and Kilmer found himself watching the rest of the movie alone "like a chump." His review? "I mean, it's so bad, it's almost good."[10]

3.2 "Schumacher was right": Social media appreciation for the Neon Knight

Even before Joel Schumacher died, social media platforms saw quite a wave of "appreciation" discourse dedicated towards the director and his impact on the Batman character. In 2015, the suggestively titled "Joel Schumacher Was Right" fan page was created on Facebook; a general description of that community explicitly stated: "This is a Joel Schumacher appreciation page." Over the years, the community practiced exactly that, recognizing Joel Schumacher's achievement by sharing specific scenes or stills, largely from his Batman films, uploading all sorts of fan-generated content (graphic art, remade movie posters, memorabilia collections, and mash-ups, combining earlier publicity content with other visual material, including depictions styled on *Batman: The Animated Series* or film posters for the 2022 *The Batman* by Matt Reeves redone to resemble the *Batman Forever* equivalent), posting information about new merchandise, and comments about the films. The Joel Schumacher Was Right social media circle—obviously structured as a "congregation" of Neon Knight's believers and disciples—was later followed by a more "generic" appreciation community established in January 2020. The Joel Schumacher Fan Page greeted users as follows:

> Welcome everybody to the fan page dedicated to my favorite director of all times: JOEL SCHUMACHER! Here you will find pictures, movie scenes, trailers, soundtracks, trivia and everything related to this amazing and eclectic director, whose filmography has touched on almost every genre of cinema: comedy, horror, comics, action, musical, drama, fantasy, thriller and romantic movies. ... His amazing career spans also through music videos and tv serials and it confirms the fact that Joel Schumacher is one of the most eclectic director of all times! JOEL SCHUMACHER: ONE DIRECTOR, A THOUSAND STORIES![11]

Dedicated exclusively to Schumacher, these two accounts were supported by the Batman Burton/Schumacher Saga fan page (2020), another attempt to build an appreciation and nostalgia-driven habitat which combined the legacies of the Burtonverse and Schumacherverse as a joint venture celebrating the entirety of the Noir-tmare Knight and the Neon Knight material as well as their conceptual derivatives.

Outside Facebook, other online resources and venues were created by Neon Knight fans and followers with Schumacher's legacy in mind. Here, one cannot fail to mention two of the most invested websites and YouTube channels run by Neil Rickatson: www.1995Batman.com (launched in February 2018) and www.1997Batman.com (launched in June 2020), dedicated to the respective Batman films. The official description of Rickatson's documentary undertaking reads: "Welcome to 1995Batman.com. A website devoted to the 1995 Joel Schumacher film *Batman Forever*. The aim of this site is to document, share and preserve as much paraphernalia to do with the film and I'll be posting vintage magazine articles, video segments, movie merchandise reviews and more over the coming years."[12] Rickatson's effort is an impressive project, aiming to provide a highly diverse and insightful look at Neon Knight-related items and texts, including detailed discussions about specific action figures from Kenner and all kinds of additional merchandise (including figure mugs by Applause, playing cards by US Playing Card Company, and detailed product reviews, describing for instance *Batman Forever*'s Batboat model from Eaglemoss' Batman Automobilia collection). Specific concepts and/or editions of Schumacher's films are even more astutely explored in Rickatson's comments about the possible final form and substance of the "Schumacher's Cut." Not unlike a genuine curator, the author collects and showcases all media/press coverage of Schumacher's Batman over the years. This committed and highly acclaimed endeavor certainly qualifies as one of the most important and comprehensive attempts at establishing an "appreciation" discourse devoted to Schumacher; Rickatson's 1995 Batman YouTube channel with 1,800 subscribers is his most meaningful accomplishment.

Besides such Schumacher-oriented online environments, there are numerous other individual posts, comments, video essays, and online discussions that may be identified as substantial elements of the discourse through which Joel Schumacher and his artistic legacy are appreciated. In an overview of such content, it would be worthwhile to describe the main categories or discursive patterns, so as to reveal the most significant points in the debate and, consequently, highlight the main assets of the director's artistic "unconventionalism" which produced the striking interpretation of Batman as the Neon Knight. Looking at the online appreciation discourse, one can distinguish three main conceptual paths which serve online debaters, commentators, and everyday users to articulate their fondness, memories, and positive assessments of the elements in Schumacher's films: "the Neon Knight in personal memory," "Batman's Neon Knight depiction," and "the Neon Knight's style," all of which display the interesting transformation of the once-ridiculed aspects of Joel Schumacher's Batman into highly regarded characteristics involved in this compelling and—as some argue—necessary attempt to reimagine the Dark Knight.

Shortly after Joel Schumacher's death was officially announced on June 22, 2020, Facebook pages dedicated to the director's oeuvre published their official condolences and posts from individual users, expressing their sadness at his passing. The Joel Schumacher Was Right page posted the following:

> This 2020 is an hard year, everyone know that. But that's the bad news that we didn't want to give on this page, this year or in any other. Joel Schumacher has passed away. This page was created by people that love him, his movies and his peculiar way of doing art. We are speechless, Joel's art was a huge part of our life, and the experience of his movies will ever be with us. The world of cinema lose a great man, and he'll be sadly missed. Safe passage Joel. You'll be always right. ♡

Subsequent eulogies made across social networks in the wake of the tragic news became an opportunity for Schumacher's fans to manifest their belief in his artistic visions of 1995 and 1997. Just as the text cited above, the adherents of the Neon Knight sought to reiterate the good points of that particular approach, informed as they were by their own memories and preferences associated with that portrayal of the Dark Knight. A user of the Facebook group Batman Burton/Schumacher Saga commented:

> I would have watched a third Schumacher movie with Batgirl and the bigger cave. Tone down the colors a little and it would have been great. I prefer the Schumacher movies over TDK. I don't need a realistic Batman movie. I'm sorry he got a lot of hate for his movies even though there were others

involved in making the films. I'm sorry that he had to battle cancer for a long time. I'm happy that he's no longer in pain and I hope he's in a good place. He leaves behind several enjoyable movies. He will be missed.[13]

Interestingly, the comments appreciative of Schumacher's Batmen underscore the crucial elements of these movies which—according to the authors—were missing in the later features, especially in Christopher Nolan's *The Dark Knight* Trilogy, a work widely considered the most contrary to Schumacher's by virtue of being too "realistic" and not "fun." This preference for the Neon duology over Nolan's Dark Knight films was reflected in a number of other Facebook comments posted in groups such as Batman Forever, an official channel dedicated to Schumacher's first Bat-project. On June 23, 2022, a short note—"RIP to the one and only Joel Schumacher. Thank you for all the movie magic you brought into our lives!"[14]—was followed by expressions of attachment to Schumacher's work, at the expense of the generally more respectable visions of Nolan or Reeves. Some were quite unequivocal: "I prefer Joel's Batman movies to Nolan's. Batman should be fun not arty. R.I.P. Joel,"[15] whereas the opinion that *Batman & Robin* was the worst cinematic portrayal of the Dark Knight, made in the context of the 2022 *The Batman*, was countered with: "Not the worst. I like it more than the new *The Batman*."[16]

The online discourse in "the Neon Knight in personal memory" category features some highly individual admissions which mention specific and idiosyncratic practices of watching, collecting, or discovering Schumacher's interpretation as a valuable or even substantial text, one that had an impact on the general attitude towards the Batman phenomenon or social issues which were not strictly Batman-related. For instance, in the previously mentioned Batman Forever thread, one user admitted that the film's bright and neon-driven interpretation had a quasi-therapeutic effect in their case:

> Rest In Peace Joel. I would like to personally send this message to send my thoughts as I have mild autism and your Batman movies have entertained myself and many of my friends, some of them with more severe difficulties and thus find the other movies too dark for them to watch. Well done to everyone involved in Batman Forever and Batman & Robin.[17]

In fact, the discourse of "personal memory" that surrounds Joel Schumacher's Batman films includes a considerable amount of more or less candid disclosures about specific moments or periods in one's youth in which the appreciation for the Neon Knight developed, mediated by a number of various products or platforms that nurtured their interest in Schumacher's work. Aside from the condolence and appreciation posts, this is well evinced in the broad selection of the Neon Knight-related archival material, including classic television commercials, VHS promos, and action figure/video game marketing. Still available for viewing, they offer interesting insights into "the Neon Knight in personal memory" category. For the sake of example, one could name the comments section under the commercial for the notorious *Batman Forever The Game* uploaded to YouTube. To a fair extent, the commenters praise both the video game—despite its bad reputation amongst gamers—and the film which it accompanied: "Childhood Memories. I know the Movie wasn't amazing but whenIa kid you don't realise how bad films etc but seeing this advertise with the song on the VHS just Nostalgic to me."[18] The game commercial appears to trigger a "nostalgic view" of the textual content compounded with an equally fond approach towards the material form of Schumacher's Batman, remembered as an element of the home release of *Batman Forever*. Specifically, one viewer comments: "I had Batman Forever on VHS as a child and this advert used to play before the movie started. I loved it so much!"[19]

Given that the film as such and the associated merchandise (which implies engaging with action figures or video games) appear to merge in the discourse of "the Neon Knight in personal memory," one should also consider the most recent content posted on social media and video platforms referencing the still-produced *Batman Forever* and *Batman & Robin* merchandise. This is because it continues to affect individual approaches towards the classic material in both films. Meaningfully titled "Was it really that bad?," an in-depth discussion concerning the reception of *Batman Forever* on the popular YouTube channel Superhero Stuff You Should Know manifests that peculiar amalgam of film experience and transmediatic participation in the overall phenomenon of Joel Schumacher's 1995 film: "It was 1995 when this movie came out and this was kinda the first time when we were of the age to see the hype of it …. Around the 94 [sic] or so they had the Warner Brothers' stores … and I just remember being a kid and wandering around and they had a huge screen showing stuff and then suddenly they've just showed the "Batman Forever" trailer …. This was my second most viewed VHS tape and this is probably my first live action batman I saw in a theatre …. I remember having a lot of the figures."[20] Likewise, the contribution of the films themselves is explicitly recognized, as the author of the video-essay "The Bizarre & Impressive Games of Batman Forever" takes a fresh look at the legacy of *Batman Forever* in that area, highlighting the creator's approach in the introduction: "Now I think it's about time to analyze the video games based on the movie and see if they're actually worth playing and hopefully provide a bigger picture on the Joel Schumacher world of Gotham as I find it to be the most appealing looking Gotham of all versions we've been introduced to throughout the years."[21]

Within the "the Neon Knight's depiction" category, one also readily distinguishes an acknowledgement motif which frequently recurs in online discussions and celebratory videos. The two actors who played Schumacher's Neon Knights in 1995 and 1997 (Val Kilmer and George Clooney) are argued to be valuable conceptual additions to the prevalent Dark Knight formula; importantly, their Batmen proved meaningful for many fans on a personal level. The author of the aforementioned "Was it really that bad?" pays a fair tribute to Kilmer's 1995 portrayal as a significant character progression with respect to what had been envisioned by Tim Burton and delivered by Michael Keaton:

> I like that Kilmer is the playboy Bruce Wayne type. … As Batman he still plays it like Michael Keaton did it. … He's a more talky version than a Keaton's version. … He just seems a little bit more intelligent …. Maybe the perfect combination for the 90's Batman is actually Kilmer …. This Batman feels more like a comic book superhero than the Burton's ones.[22]

Various other critiques of Kilmer's version of Batman/Bruce Wayne demonstrate a similar pattern, stating that his idea for the character needs to be re-evaluated because it is more comic book-like as well as more emotional and human than Burton's. The video-essay "Batman Forever: The Best Batman Movie?" makes a significant assertion about Kilmer's "humanity," referring to the plotline involving the mock suicide incident staged by The Riddler in Wayne's company:

> Later after talking about the apparent suicide with the commissioner, Bruce Wayne goes on to show his human side by ensuring the family get full benefits regardless of suicide not being covered by the company policies. I think this is a beautiful and very human touch which is easily glossed over as it's such a throwaway line which sits in the background to Wayne getting his first riddle.[23]

What is interesting in today's opinions regarding the once disparaged first Batman by Schumacher is that they share appreciation for its "emotional" and more "caring" interpretation. Just as in the previous quote, many modern commentators find Kilmer's iteration of the Neon Knight to have been a logical step forward given Keaton's relentless and brutal hero, and a refreshing take on the rarely seen romantic side of Batman, unfolding in the onscreen interaction between Kilmer's Wayne and Nicole Kidman's Dr. Chase Meridian. With the introduction of Dr. Chase Meridian as the main love interest of Kilmer's Neon Knight in *Batman Forever*, it has been conjectured that the main story of the 1995 feature shows Batman seeking balance or a stable course in his life, a goal he ultimately achieves in the course of onscreen events. Having decided to place Batman in the position of self-rivalry and a paradoxical love triangle involving Wayne being in love with Chase who falls for Batman as a Wayne's alter ego, Schumacher introduced a somewhat unfamiliar theme of Batman trying to find mental and emotional healing and work through his painful memories and trauma, which are no longer a driving force but an obstacle. In the superhero's crowning line—"I'm both Bruce Wayne and Batman. Not because I have to be. Now, because I choose to be"—Schumacher radically changes the status quo of the Dark Knight, abandoning the brooding characterization in favor of a character who is fully reconciled with himself. That fundamental shift and the attempt to have Batman progress in terms of personal growth is another motif widely praised by Schumacher's fans today, who seem to have higher regard for that unorthodoxy within the Dark Knight standard. This is evinced in the meaningfully titled "101 Great Things about Batman and Robin," a video-essay which discusses numerous assets of the film, emphasizing the introduction of the Brighter Knight as the most valuable character development:

> I do like that this movie has a focus on family. The ones that you're born to and the ones that you choose over time. When trying to make these movies follow one steady narrative … is not easy task. One could see this as evolution of the Bruce Wayne character. Starting off as an isolated loner who shuns the public and any chance of a personal life. Over the years come into his own accept his own public persona except his life outside the cape and cowl and how he's out there taking in orphans and starting a family of his own. It's nice to see this growth.[24]

When George Clooney replaced Val Kilmer as the finally untraumatized Neon Knight in the 1997 *Batman & Robin*, his Bruce Wayne showed no traits of a brooding or depressed vigilante. That portrayal also receives a substantial amount of renewed interest today, as many fans see it as direct continuation of the 1995 narrative. With Clooney's performance being frequently appreciated along the lines of "It's in a way refreshing to see a more heroic dark knight,"[25] one can identify two other tropes of re-evaluation which try to vindicate the previously deprecated elements in *Batman & Robin*, i.e., Clooney's family-friendly Dad Knight instead of a cool loner and the widely criticized sexualization of Batman's outfit. The apparently provocative presentation "101 Great Things about Batman and Robin" offers an interesting look at the starring role which, dispraised as dull and flat, is redefined using the following arguments:

> I do think that as a public persona as Bruce Wayne goes, George Clooney was a great choice. Whether by design, accident or coincidence, you can completely buy George Clooney being a smarmy billionaire playboy. As a matter of fact I would say that's the role George was born to play. … I think the scenes in which we see him as Bruce, especially when he's out in public really work for the character and really work in favor of the movie.[26]

There is increasing appreciation for the "humanness" of the character—already introduced with Kilmer's protagonist—which manifests in the actions of the 1997 Batman and his radically different treatment of the villains, especially compared with the Burton films. This is noted by the authors of *Superhero Stuff You Should Know* as they ask "Was it really that bad?" regarding Schumacher's second endeavor: "The ending is kinda underrated when it comes to Mr Freeze's arc…. I think nobody talks about this is the fact that batman actually helps Freeze becomes Victor Freeze again…. He rehabilitates a villain … and we haven't even seen it in really any of the movie since."[27]

On the wave of appreciation for the Brighter Knight that Joel Schumacher developed in his Batman duology, even the most controversial and un-Batman-like elements in his two movies are redeemed to some degree, because fans see them as valuable variations on the otherwise "static" character of Batman. With Clooney exonerated as a more optimistic and hope-bringing Knight, it should not come as a surprise that even the "tangible" aspects of his performance—the rubber nipples, no less—were also reconsidered in terms of their effect on reducing the macho ingredient in the Dark Knight's depiction. That achievement is praised in "Batman & Robin is a Misunderstood Masterpiece," which concludes that the "sexualized" look of Clooney's Batman was an act of an artistic subversion:

> To many fanboys Bruce Wayne/Batman is supposed to be this super macho manly man fighting crime. And as such many men idolize him. … So there's no doubt that seeing their favorite male character being filmed the way that women are was too much for their hetero minds to handle …. Joel Schumacher flipped that trope on its head …. Nobody looks like that. At least, no one with a healthy relationship with their body. So why not make an absurd costume that creates that body for them?[28]

As regards "Batman's Neon Knight depiction," it could hardly have been expected that essentially all those features of Schumacher's Neon Knight that were branded as inferior—such as visual depiction, greater emphasis on socialization, and the untraumatized psyche—are embraced by fans who may recognize them as "different" yet gratifying elaborations of the otherwise-fixed Batman lore. Hence, it is not as shocking today to encounter such assertions as "Schumacher understood Batman's character better than Burton …. And it's because Burton doesn't give a fuck about Batman,"[29] from which it follows that Schumacher's Neon Knight is a rightful creation among Batman's transmediatic and trans-aesthetic implementations. That being said, one has to remember that the more favorable notions about Schumacher's take on the character are to a fair extent fueled by individual, subjective preference for the distinctive visual concept that Schumacher reified in his Batmen.

In any case, whatever has been said about Schumacher's films recently in any format and media, it never fails to address one particular aspect, regardless of whether such articulations are interested in praising or bashing the duology: by and large, the one single thing that seems to elicit positive recognition nowadays is the look of both *Batman Forever* and *Batman & Robin*—the neon-filled, colorful, and easily absurd style that has become so emblematic of those films over the years. Significantly enough, it has been found meaningful in a discussion about the differences between the cinematic and comic book adaptations of *Batman & Robin*: "One thing this comic is missing is the appearance of Schumacher's Gotham city with all those neon lights vivid colors."[30] As previously observed, the "living comic book" aesthetic was absolutely essential to Schumacher's efforts to construct the onscreen visual narrative. Perhaps unwittingly, this is palpably reflected in the present-day reactions across social media, in which the phrases "living comic book," "like a comic book," or "just as in comic books" are ubiquitous by means of which the fans and commenters try to convey their own fascination with that particular style. In an assessment entitled "Joel Schumacher's Batman Forever is a Flawed Masterpiece," the author states right at the start that "There are beautifully-done set pieces that bring Gotham to life and on top of that there are still moments that visually feels like a comic book such as the Riddler's headquarters towards the end of Batman Forever. … Schumacher perfectly captures the essence of what a Batman movie should have looked like during the 90's era."[31] The same enthusiastic tones are heard in "101 Great Things about Batman and Robin," which speaks in highly positive terms about Schumacher's neons, which effectively enrich Batman's portrayal:

> Schumacher's Gotham does have a personality on its own. A massive, mostly crime-driven city, where an over-the-top cartoony criminal underworld takes center stage. Where gangs look like they're better suited at a rave. Where giant statues of muscular men are intertwined in buildings architecture. Where it's mostly night 24 hours of the day and neon signs light

the city streets. I don't love this take on Gotham ... but I do appreciate it ....
It's not my Gotham City but it is Joel Schumacher's and I dig it.³²

And also in the comment from "Batman Forever – The Best & Worst of Batman on Film" produced by Cortex Videos: "Cinematographer Stephen Goldblatt uses tilts and moves his camera with a certain flair, stamping his style across the film in ways we simply don't see in most superhero films today. And production designer Barbara Ling gives every point of Gotham City the moody atmosphere and neon art it deserves."³³

The "Neon Knight's style" current in the discourse, whose presence in social media is quite considerable today, is an element that brings together the two other dominant themes in this renewed appreciation for Schumacher's Neon Knight. Combined with openly manifested approval for the more optimistic depiction of Batman and deeply personal memories of the first exposure to Schumacher's films, the partiality for the vivid and visually "aggressive" interpretation of Batman's world fuses into one with the Neon Knight's essence of an aesthetically and emotionally brighter embodiment of the Dark Knight, one that finds its faithful and committed audience (as the meaningful conclusion of the *Batman & Robin*'s "Was It Really That Bad?" discussion on the Superhero Stuff You Should Know channel suggests: "I think we remember it being atrocious because everyone else said it was atrocious ... we kinda thought we hated it because the rest of the Internet said so"³⁴). Despite all former or recent concerns that Schumacher's films do not feature the "right" iterations of the protagonist, the substantial evidence from the various online activities involving numerous persons leads to a contrary but inevitable conclusion, namely that the Neon Knight is indeed as valid as the more "traditional" versions of the hero; in some cases, it may even be more "central" and "canon" than his more conservative renditions. By way of a closing remark, these deliberations may be summed up by a final, compelling quote from Schumacher's believers:

> We already have so many mediums that lack any positive emotion, that dive deep into the lore of Batman that have the blandest and simplest of color palettes, that presents the typical brooding billionaire-bachelor that we think of when we think of Batman, and guess what ... when I think of Batman and Robin I think of the heart, I think of the neon over-the-top

colors, the ridiculous eccentric self-aware supervillains, the beautiful set pieces and most importantly a Batman movie that makes me smile and laugh. … The humility is what makes these movies memorable. … Let's have fun with it and let's have a good time, because why not?[35]

Notes

1. Josh Shin, "Batman Forever Is STILL The Dark Knight's Most Underrated Movie," CBR.com, June 24, 2020, https://www.cbr.com/batman-forever-dark-knight-most-underrated-movie/.
2. Rosie Knight, "Why Batman and Robin Is the Underrated Gem of The Batman Franchise," nerdist.com, June 16, 2017, https://nerdist.com/article/why-batman-and-robin-is-the-underrated-gem-of-the-batman-franchise/?fbclid=IwAR2rmOm2DV63-wZFCzKDb-x8OLPWBetOjS4Bym6STBJrpapPIvKHLp948ig.
3. Josh Shin, "Batman Forever Is STILL The Dark Knight's Most Underrated Movie," CBR.com, June 24, 2020, https://www.cbr.com/batman-forever-dark-knight-most-underrated-movie/.
4. Brecken Hunter Wellborn, "Why 'Batman and Robin's' Poison Ivy Is the Definitive Camp Supervillain," collider.com, June 20, 2022, https://collider.com/batman-and-robin-poison-ivy-best-camp-supervillain/?fbclid=IwAR0nylZz-In9KdAJTLebLsdvkRHKPaUo3aWs5TC-C6DZaQuv5lXeNXUE1QE.
5. Jon Holmes, "Riddle Me This … was Jim Carrey as The Riddler a Good Performance?," movieweb.com, May 13, 2022, https://movieweb.com/jim-carrey-as-the-riddler/.
6. Christian Colby Eltell, "Batman Forever Is Actually a Better Batman Movie than People Remember," gamerant.com, July 4, 2021, https://gamerant.com/batman-forever-better-movie-people-believe/.
7. Rosie Knight, "Why Batman and Robin is the Underrated Gem of The Batman Franchise," nerdist.com, June 16, 2017, https://nerdist.com/article/why-batman-and-robin-is-the-underrated-gem-of-the-batman-franchise/?fbclid=IwAR2rmOm2DV63-wZFCzKDb-x8OLPWBetOjS4Bym6STBJrpapPIvKHLp948ig.
8. DocLathropBrown, "In Defense of the Neon Knight: Where Schumacher Succeeded," batman-online.com, July 26, 2012, https://www.batman-online.com/features/2012/7/26/in-defense-of-the-neon-knight-where-schumachers-batman-succeeded?fbclid=IwAR3NVzobwdd80CaOG1O3zArmpivuBYj-nrtKh8FAlhcrJ-qW_wlNw29x50g.

9. Martin's Movie Review, "A Critical Reevaluation – Batman & Robin," martinsmoviereview.blogspot.com, June 20, 2017, http://martinsmoviereview.blogspot.com/2017/06/a-critical-reavaluation-batman-robin.html.
10. David Crow, "Val Kilmer on Batman Forever: 'It's So Bad, It's Almost Good,'" denofgeek.com, August 30, 2021, https://www.denofgeek.com/movies/val-kilmer-batman-forever-so-bad-its-good/.
11. Joel Schumacher Fan Page, Facebook, January 4, 2020, https://www.facebook.com/JoelSchumacherFanPage/posts/pfbid02NjkHHg9v3rb9ZibEYHAo2eUZ4RNDKaoACJtKQ1YrfiPXRpRNRtRiFdnSYmG7E5nol.
12. https://www.1995batman.com/.
13. Batman Forever Facebook Group, Facebook, June 22, 2020, https://www.facebook.com/photo/?fbid=3071666406287240&set=g.372541543461506.
14. Batman Forever, Facebook, June 23, 2020, https://www.facebook.com/BatmanForeverFilm/photos/a.257946084382999/1627166220794305.
15. Ibid.
16. Batman-online.com, Facebook, July 10, 2022, https://www.facebook.com/batmanonlinecom/photos/a.661112673898825/5837106376299403/.
17. Batman Forever, Facebook, June 23, 2020, https://www.facebook.com/BatmanForeverFilm/photos/a.257946084382999/1627166220794305.
18. SpacedCobraTV, "Batman Forever: The Game Commercial," YouTube, 2009, https://www.youtube.com/watch?v=nn5ftuJOTew&list=PLvOhZIQVv6hBvq8nIHmaVMfZP0ya5a0i7&index=5.
19. Ibid.
20. Superhero Stuff You Should Know, "Batman Forever – Was It Really That Bad?," YouTube, 2020, https://www.youtube.com/watch?v=wyqnVBbYBHQ&list=PLvOhZIQVv6hBvq8nIHmaVMfZP0ya5a0i7&index=34.
21. ScorePN, "The Bizarre & Impressive Games of Batman Forever," YouTube, January 23, 2022, https://www.youtube.com/watch?v=P0Ue5zUzcIw&list=-PLCSfG4gkgW-AowfaR4VmvaK92CBdvlaeD&index=3.
22. ScorePN, "The Bizzarre & Impressive Games of Batman Forever," YouTube, 2022, https://www.youtube.com/watch?v=wyqnVBbYBHQ&list=PLvOhZIQVv6hBvq8nIHmaVMfZP0ya5a0i7&index=37.
23. Channel Pup, "Batman Forever: The Best Batman Movie?," YouTube, 2020, https://www.youtube.com/watch?v=PHBco-Drnss&list=PLvOhZIQVv6hBvq8nIHmaVMfZP0ya5a0i7&index=34.

24   Vee Infuso, "101 Great Things about Batman And Robin (Part One)," YouTube, 2022, https://www.youtube.com/watch?v=JYrv-ZxQsgY&t=4s&ab_channel=VeeInfuso.

25   Diamondbolt, "Batman & Robin: The Worst Superhero Movie (w/ Markscaper)," YouTube, 2021, https://www.youtube.com/watch?v=GtjJNbpsSOY&list=PLvOhZIQVv6hBvq8nIHmaVMfZP0ya5a0i7&index=59.

26   Vee Infuso, "101 Great Things about Batman and Robin (Part One)," YouTube, 2022, https://www.youtube.com/watch?v=JYrv-ZxQsgY&t=1432s&ab_channel=VeeInfuso.

27   Superhero Stuff you Should Know, "Was It Really That Bad? Looking Back on Batman and Robin," YouTube, 2021, https://www.youtube.com/watch?v=Ts3cFlU3o4k&list=PLvOhZIQVv6hBvq8nIHmaVMfZP0ya5a0i7&index=40.

28   ModernGurlz, "Batman & Robin is a Misunderstood Masterpiece 🦇💋❄️," YouTube, 2021, https://www.youtube.com/watch?v=5J8MFACA4v8&list=PLvOhZIQVv6hBvq8nIHmaVMfZP0ya5a0i7&index=106.

29   Superhero Stuff you Should Know, "Was It Really That Bad? Looking Back on Batman and Robin," YouTube, 2021, https://www.youtube.com/watch?v=Ts3cFlU3o4k&list=PLvOhZIQVv6hBvq8nIHmaVMfZP0ya5a0i7&index=40.

30   ScorePN, "Differences in Batman & Robin (1997) Movie vs Comic," YouTube, 2022, https://www.youtube.com/watch?v=JuHA4mXuNXU&list=PLCSfG4gkgW-AowfaR4VMvaK92CBdvlaeD&index=7.

31   IDontBeatGames, "Joel Schumacher's Batman Forever Is a Flawed Masterpiece," YouTube, 2022, https://www.youtube.com/watch?v=0S–S_nG50o&list=PLvOhZIQVv6hBvq8nIHmaVMfZP0ya5a0i7&index=62.

32   Vee Infuso, "101 Great Things about Batman and Robin (Part One)," YouTube, 2022, https://www.youtube.com/watch?v=JYrv-ZxQsgY&t=4s&ab_channel=VeeInfuso.

33   Cortex Videos, "BATMAN FOREVER – The Best & Worst of Batman on Film," YouTube, 2022, https://www.youtube.com/watch?v=hQnvg2dcOMg&t=693s&ab_channel=CortexVideos.

34   Superhero Stuff you Should Know, "Was It Really That Bad? Looking Back on Batman and Robin," YouTube, 2021, https://www.youtube.com/watch?v=Ts3cFlU3o4k&t=3048s&ab_channel=SuperheroStuffYouShouldKnow.

35   IDontBeatGames, "Joel Schumacher's Batman & Robin Isn't An Awful Batman Movie," YouTube, 2022, https://www.youtube.com/watch?v=35jw6mQTnKo&list=PLvOhZIQVv6hBvq8nIHmaVMfZP0ya5a0i7&index=108.

Closing remarks or "We're going to need a bigger cave"

Despite the negative overtone of Kevin Feige's assertion with which this analysis started, it is quite evident today that the anti-Schumacher trend is reversing, both in the reception of the audience, with their newly found appreciation, and in the rising wave in modern superhero filmmaking, which seems to draw increasingly on the Neon-saturated idea of the "living comic book" instead of the post-Nolan visualization of caped crusaders in their practical or realistic costumes. Even within Feige's own conceptual oeuvre of the Marvel Cinematic Universe, the most eminent recent achievements appear to have more in common with the over-the-top instances of the "aesthetic of artifice," once rejected by the MCU's main man. Financially successful and artistically acclaimed, both James Gunn's *Guardians of the Galaxy* features from 2014 and 2017, alongside Taika Waititi's take on Thor, the God of Thunder in *Thor Ragnarok* (2018) and *Thor: Love and Thunder* (2022), are genuine continuators of Joel Schumacher's concept of making comic books come alive through the aesthetic of excess and overall visual brightness. In the preface to the sumptuous album *The Art of "Guardians of the Galaxy"* by Marie Javins, James Gunn himself highlights the core idea of bringing the comic book essence of the *Guardians of the Galaxy* to the big screen by means of openly overdone and stylized production. According to Gunn,

> At first it was mostly a visual thing. ... *Alien* and *Blade Runner* are groundbreaking films, but so many science fiction films have been entombed by them, relying on darkness and grittiness to make them "real". ... *Guardians of the Galaxy* would be about color, and life. In-your-face over-the-top, unrepentant COLOR. We would rescue the aesthetics of pulpy science fiction films from the fifties and sixties.
>
> (Javins 2014: Foreword)

Indeed, it would not be that difficult to replace the title of Gunn's space superhero epic with Schumacher's duology and find the very same inspiration and intention, which consists of amplifying light elements in the fairly narrow, pre-established visual paradigm of the genre in question. This intention flourishes in the sequel to the 2014 Marvel cosmic blockbuster, as the director once again openly affirms his reliance on even brighter themes and imagery: "I wanted it to be more explosively colorful, more outlandishly science fiction, and more rooted in pulp art and the space-opera films … I put together a lookbook of visual cues containing old *Amazing Stories* covers, Al Williamson and Jim Starlin art … frames from the 1980's *Flash Gordon* and Wong-Kar Wai films" (Johnston 2017: Foreword), adding a significant remark about one of the film's locations: "And like Las Vegas, often there's neon—it's a lure to get people in" (139).

References to aesthetic "exaggeration," manifesting in the surreal geographies and set designs, outlandish color palette, and expressive filmmaking techniques are also often made with respect to Taika Waititi's vision for a high-value Marvel asset in the shape of two *Thor* installments, which derive substantial inspiration from Jack Kirby's drawing style. Eleni Roussos' behind-the-scenes look at *Thor Ragnarok* in *The Art of "Thor Ragnarok,"* features a quote from Kevin Feige who admits that it played no mean role:

> in this particular movie, Taika had an idea to just really make it a tribute and take it as close as we could get to his design style from the comics and not just use them for tonal inspiration. And the lines that you see are in many cases taken directly from his panels. It's almost a surreal experience walking around, as if we had finally, after so many years, stepped into a Jack Kirby drawing.
>
> (Roussos 2018: 177)

There are more projects that seem very keen on maintaining this unrealistic and opulent vibe of onscreen superhero exploits in the recent DC catalog, with the most obvious example being James Wan's *Aquaman* (2018), which follows the same pattern of exploiting artifice over reality. When the creators of that hit blockbuster took advantage of the bioluminescent aesthetic to depict the underwater kingdom of Atlantis, their goal was not to concretize the "practicality" of the vehicles used by the Atlantians or their abodes but go for the extravagant aspect, drenched in underwater neons: "As a result, everything in Atlantis shimmers and glows. ... Functionality was as important as visual flair" (Avila 2018: 78).

Still, even in the latest reintroduction of Batman's character in Matt Reeves' *The Batman* (2022), there were perceptible nods towards the once disavowed legacy of the ridiculed Neon Knight. For a time, Christopher Nolan's visually "practical" *Dark Knight* Trilogy predominated, with its almost semi-documentary style and Chicago-like Gotham City, but *The Batman* seems to depart from that stylistic formula. It does share certain Nolanesque conceptual solutions in terms of imagery, but it opts for a much more flamboyant visual and musical setting. As Matt Reeves' entry into the franchise was discussed in various media, Schumacher's adherents would note that it was prominently reminiscent of the 1995 and 1997 idea of aesthetic excess. While praising the work of Greg Fraser, the cinematographer in *The Batman*, it was commonly observed that with his touch "Gotham feels like a living, breathing gothic city with neon signage and streetlights."[1] Indeed, the 2022 Gotham City demonstrates some similarities with Schumacher's over-aestheticized, neon urban jungle, deliberately exploiting light patterns and neon blasts to achieve the expressionistic feel of a city space that has no interest in becoming too artistically limited due to the requirements of realism. In the artbook to accompany the film, director Matt Reeves refers to the expressionistic lighting techniques to explain its nearly aggressive effect on the viewer's perception: "Light has always been a critical and deeply emotional part of the image to me .... And Greg is the master of light. ... We used these wonderfully imperfect, anamorphic lenses .... Greg's whole approach is about finding ways to bring texture into the overly clean digital image so it has a much more film-like quality" (Field 2022: 192). The same applies to the auditory aspect, as the sound design and score by Michael Giacchino also pursue this immersion-through-exaggeration approach: "almost nothing you hear in a film like this is a reflection of reality. The sound is almost entirely impressionistic and expressionistic. The idea is to create a sound that feels right to the audience not one that would be accurate if closely examined."[2]

All the above examples may be presumed to reflect a triumphant return of the "neon" type of filmmaking, in which creators explore theatricality and graphic-like possibilities of showing superhero exploits onscreen, rather than restricting them to "probable" interpretations of the originally improbable figures and heroes. This "aesthetic of artifice" manifested in Schumacher's depictions of Batman finds new applications today, as a number of filmmakers readily embrace cinematic comic book-ness as a multisensory experience, amplifying all audiovisual components to obtain an eye-riveting, pictorial pageant. However, the Neon Knight left an imprint on more essential ingredients of the modern spectacles such as *Guardians of the Galaxy* or *The Batman*. These aesthetically post-neon features appear to follow in the trespassing footsteps of Schumacher, going against the expectations nurtured by the erstwhile formula of the superhero story.

It is thus no coincidence that Gunn's space opera is more a fully developed family story than a typical Caped-Crusader-themed narrative in a cosmic setting, while its main protagonist, Peter Quill, is a somewhat helpless man-child—despite his adequately "manly" physique—and profound dependency on his relationship with other members of the Guardian squad. Likewise, Waititi's reimagined Thor is remote from the original depictions of the mythical figure, shifting towards more personally tragic as well as comedic, undermining the "seriousness" of the character. Moreover, Waititi decided to take Thor's character beyond the realm of typical superhero affairs and give him a foster daughter to raise in the unexpected finale of the 2022 *Thor: Love & Thunder*. This closing character twist and the overall unbalanced tone of Waititi's second *Thor* feature drew some backlash from the fans, and it is striking how closely this resembles the concerns regarding Schumacher's earlier "meddling" with Batman's personality by de-traumatizing it in *Batman and Robin*. Finally, the latest iteration of the Dark Knight conceived by Reeves conveys an implicit commentary about the ineffective fixation with brooding characters, as the hero's journey in *The Batman* starts with Bruce Wayne defining himself as a "nocturnal animal" who brutally preys on Gotham City's bandits and ends with the same Batman working hand in hand with the city's enforcement during the daytime, as he helps a young woman by taking her gently by the hand. With the sequels to Reeves' *The Batman* already announced, there is a strong possibility that the subsequent stories will move even further away from the Dark Knight, making new attempts to broaden Batman's conceptual scope to—metaphorically—paint his iconic cowl in a different color palette as a token of willingness to move once again towards the Bright Knight interpretation.

The line cited in the title of this conclusion originates from the very last scene of Joel Schumacher's *Batman & Robin*, a heart-warming and highly significant shot featuring Batman, Robin, and the newly inducted Batgirl, who now form an official alliance and partnership. Alfred comments astutely: "We're going to need a bigger cave." In line with what I have tried to show in my analysis, the final message from Schumacher's feature may also be perceived as a much more meta-textual remark on Batman—and superhero-centered narratives, since the director's personal need for artistic trespassing, manifested clearly in those two materializations of the Neon Knight. Schumacher's striving for an aesthetic and conceptual "opening" of the Batman lore as well as expansion of the visual forms and character modalities ultimately translates into a call for encouraging and accepting all possible counter-factual and/or counter-aesthetic ideas about the Batman persona. Importantly, they would thus be equally valuable and meaningful for a fair number of Bat-fans and followers who discover their very own reifications of the character in those unorthodox visions and understandings. The "bigger Batcave" creed is a powerful reminder from Schumacher to see such fictional superheroes as true "floating signifiers," entities that do not have to stick to just one primary iteration but may and should seek their unobvious variations. The outcomes may happen to be unwelcome to some, but they will be thematically progressive and culturally inclusive, finding an audience all the same. This appeal for a bigger cave that can accommodate all Batmen and Batwomen out there—whatever their shape, tone, and cowl color may be—constitutes the most crucial element of Joel Schumacher's legacy, in which his Neon Knight is a thoroughly viable proposal in the continually developing Batman phenomenon. As a result, there is still work to be done within the discourse focusing on Schumacher and his neon vigilante, as well as regarding the infinite other Knights that are already seen or will come to be seen through multiple potential readings by the creators and consumers of all related Bat-media. Since the necessity of exploring such creations as part of Batman and superhero studies is as inevitable as it is promising, one should perhaps recall the sound advice that Dr. Chase Meridian offers at the end of *Batman Forever*, Schumacher's first step to address "the need for a bigger cave": "Don't work too late."

Notes

1. Patrick Tomasso, "Why THE BATMAN is so Beautiful. A Cinematography Video Essay," YouTube, 2022, https://www.youtube.com/watch?v=STynLl-2FqU&list=PLvOhZIQVv6hBvq8nIHmaVMfZP0ya5a0i7&index=78.
2. Thomas Flight, "Why The Batman Sound is Different," YouTube, 2022, https://www.youtube.com/watch?v=_AQkQ4a1yJ8&list=PLvOhZIQVv6hBvq8nIHmaVMfZP0ya5a0i7&index=82.

Bibliography

Adamou, Christina. "Evolving Portrayals of Masculinity in Superhero Films: Hancock." In *The 21st Century Superhero: Essays on Gender, Genre and the Globalization in Film*, edited by Richard J. Gray II and Betty Kaklamanidou, 94–110. Jefferson: McFarland & Company, 2011.

Avila, Mike. *The Art and Making of "Aquaman."* San Raphael: Insight Editions, 2018.

Batman & Robin. The Official Souvenir Magazine. London: Titan Magazines, 1997.

Beard, Jim. "Such a Character: A Dissection of Two Sub-Species of Chiroptera Homo Sapiens." In *Gotham City 14 Miles. 14 Essays on Why 1960's Batman TV Series Matters*, edited by Jim Beard, 56–75. Edwardsville: Sequart, 2010.

Bennett, Tony and Janet Woollacott. *Bond and Beyond: The Political Career of a Popular Hero.* Basingstoke: Macmillan Education, 1987.

Boym, Svetlana. *The Future of Nostalgia.* New York: Basic Books, 2001.

Brooker, Will. *Batman Unmasked: Analyzing a Cultural Icon.* London: Bloomsbury, 2000.

Brooker, Will. *Hunting the Dark Knight: Twenty-First Century Batman.* London: I.B. Tauris, 2012.

Brown, Jeffrey A. *Batman and the Multiplicity of Identity: The Contemporary Comic Book Superhero as Cultural Nexus.* New York: Routledge, 2018.

Burke, Liam. *Superhero Movies.* Harpenden: Pocket Essentials, 2008.

Cohen, Michael. "Dick Tracy: In Pursuit of a Comic Book Aesthetic." In *Film and Comic Books*, edited by Ian Gordon, Mark Jancovich, and Matthew P. McAllister, 13–36. Jackson: University Press of Mississippi, 2007.

Collins, Gary. *Holy Franchise Batman! Bringing the Caped Crusader to the Screen.* London: Robert Hale, 2012.

Dixon, Wheeler Winston and Richard Graham. *A Brief History of Comic Book Movies.* London: Palgrave Macmillan, 2017.

Dondero, Jennifer. "Dark Hero Rising: How Online Batman Fandom Helped Create a Cultural Archetype." In *Fan Phenomenon: Batman*, edited by Liam Burke, 30–9. Chicago: Intellect Books, 2013.

Dudenhoeffer, Larry. *Anatomy of the Superhero Film.* London: Palgrave Macmillan, 2017.

Durand, Kevin K. "Batman's 'Canon'. Hybridity and the Interpretation of the Superhero." In *Riddle Me This, Batman! Essays on the Universe of the Dark Knight*, edited by Kevin K. Durand and Mary K. Leigh, 81–92. Jefferson: McFarland & Company, 2011.

Eco, Umberto. "The Myth of Superman." *Diacritics* 1(2) (1972): 14–22.

Eury, Michael. *Captain Action: The Original Super-Hero Action Figure*. Raleigh: TwoMorrows Publishing, 1999.

Field, James. *The Art of "The Batman."* New York: Abrams, 2022.

Fleming, Dan. *Powerplay: Toys as Popular Culture*. Manchester: Manchester University Press, 1996.

Fraga, Kristian. *Tim Burton: Interviews*. Jackson: University Press of Mississippi, 2005.

Friedenthal, Andrew. *Retcon Game. Retroactive Continuity and the Hyperlinking of America*. Jackson: University Press of Mississippi, 2017.

Friedenthal, Andrew. *The World of DC Comics*. New York: Routledge, 2019.

Garcia, Robert and Joe Desris. *Batman: A Celebration of the Classic TV Series*. London: Titan Books, 2016.

Hanley, Tim. *The Many Lives of Catwoman: The Felonious History of a Feline Fatale*. Chicago: Chicago Review Press, 2017.

Javins, Marie. *The Art of "Guardians of the Galaxy."* New York: Marvel, 2014.

Jeffries, Dru. *Comic Book Film Style: Cinema at 24 Panels per Second*. Austin: University of Texas Press, 2017.

Johnston, Jacob. *The Art of "Guardians of the Galaxy. Vol. 2."* New York: Marvel, 2017.

Kaveney, Roz. *Superheroes! Capes and Crusaders in Comics and Films*. London: I.B. Tauris, 2008.

Klock, Geoff. *How to Read Superhero Comics and Why*. New York: Continuum, 2002.

Kukkonen, Karin. "Navigating Infinite Earths." In *The Superhero Reader*, edited by Charles Hatfield, Jeet Heer, and Kent Worcester, 155–69. Jackson: University Press of Mississippi, 2013.

Mamatas, Nick. "Holy Signifier, Batman!" In *Batman Unauthorized: Vigilantes, Jokers and Heroes in Gotham City*, edited by Alan J. Porter, Chris Roberson, Jake Black, and Dennis O'Neil, 47–54. Dallas: Smart Pop, 2008.

McCloud, Scott. *Understanding Comics: The Invisible Art*. New York: Harper Collins, 1994.

Morton, Drew. *Panel to the Screen: Style, American Film and Comic Books during the Blockbuster Era*. Jackson: University Press of Mississippi, 2017.

Owczarski, Kimberly Ann. "Batman, Time Warner, and Franchise Filmmaking in the Conglomerate Era," doctoral diss., Faculty of the Graduate School of The University of Texas, USA, 2008.

Pearson, Roberta and William Uricchio. *The Many Lives of Batman: Critical Approaches to a Superhero and His Media*. New York: Routledge, 1991.

Peretti, Daniel. *Superman in Myth and Folklore*. Jackson: University Press of Mississippi, 2017.

Proctor, William. "Schrödinger's Cape: The Quantum Seriality of the Marvel Multiverse." In *Make Ours Marvel: Media Convergence and a Comics Universe*, edited by Matt Yockey, 319–46. Austin: University of Texas Press, 2017.

Pumphrey, Nicholaus. *Superman and the Bible: How the Idea of Superheroes Affects the Reading of Scripture*. Jefferson: McFarland & Company, 2019.

Reinhart, Mark S. *The Batman Filmography*. Jefferson: McFarland & Company, 2013.

Reynolds, Richard. *Super Heroes: A Modern Mythology*. Jackson: University Press of Mississippi, 1992.

Rodgers, Will. *The Ultimate Super Friends Companion*, vol. 1: *The 1970s*. New York: CreateSpace Independent Publishing Platform, 2016.

Romagnoli, Alex S. and Gian S. Pagnucci. *Enter the Superheroes: American Values, Culture and the Canon of Superhero Literature*. Lanham: Scarecrow Press, 2013.

Roussos, Eleni. *The Art of "Thor Ragnarok."* New York: Marvel, 2018.

Scivally, Bruce. *Billion Dollar Batman: A History of the Caped Crusader on Film, Radio and Television from 10 Cent Comic Book to Global Icon*. Wilmette: Henry Gray Publishing, 2011.

Singer, Michael. *Batman & Robin: The Making of the Movie*. London: Titan Books, 1997.

Singer, Michael. *Batman Forever: The Official Movie Book*. London: Mandarin Peperbacks, 1995.

Singer, Michael. *Batman Returns: The Official Movie Book*. London: Hamlyn, 1992.

Spigel, Lynn and Henry Jenkins. "Same Bat Channel, Different Bat Times: Mass Culture and Popular Memory." In *Many More Lives of Batman*, edited by Roberta Pearson, William Uricchio, and Will Brooker, 171–97. London: British Film Institute, 2015.

Wandtke, Terrence R. "Introduction: Once Upon a Time Once Again." In *The Amazing Transforming Superhero! Essays on the Revision of Characters in Comic Books, Film and Television*, edited by Terrence R. Wandtke, 5–31. Jefferson: McFarland & Company, 2007.

Wandtke, Terrence R. *The Meaning of Superhero Comic Books*. Jefferson: McFarland & Company, 2012.

Weldon, Glen. *The Caped Crusade: Batman and the Rise of Nerd Culture*. New York: Simon & Schuster Paperbacks, 2016.

Young, Matthew David. "Musical Topics in the Comic Book Superhero Film Genre," doctoral diss., Faculty of the Graduate School of The University of Texas, USA, 2013.

Index

8mm 53, 55

A Time to Kill 50, 59
Adamou, Christina 89, 137
Affleck, Ben 30
Aldis, Ben 68, 104
Alien 131
Allen, Woody 49, 102
Archie's TV Funnies 38
Avila, Mike 133, 137

Batchler, Janet 69, 95, 96, 105
Batchler [1989], Lee 69, 95, 96, 105
Batman 2, 61, 62, 63, 65, 66, 84, 85, 86, 95, 98
Batman [1966] 28, 35, 39, 40, 47, 107
Batman & Robin 1, 3–6, 9–12, 15, 34, 47, 50, 53, 59–60, 67, 73–4, 78–83, 91–2, 94–6, 98–9, 101, 103–4, 107, 109–10, 112–15, 119–20, 123–5, 128–9, 135, 137, 139
Batman Forever viii, 1–4, 6–12, 14–16, 31, 34, 47, 49–50, 58–60, 67–9, 70, 73, 75–87, 90, 93–101, 103–5, 107, 109–14, 116–17, 119–22, 125–9, 136, 139
Batman Returns 2, 42, 58, 61, 62, 63, 64, 65, 66, 78, 84, 85, 95, 103, 104, 105, 139
Batman and the Super 7 39
Batman v Superman: Dawn of Justice 22
Batman: The Animated Series 48, 100, 109, 116
Beard, Jim 23, 137
Beatty, Warren 72, 73
Bennett, Tony 20, 137
Birds of Prey or the Fantabulous Emancipation of One Harley Quinn 3
Blade Runner 131
Borges, Jorge Luis 27
Borrelli, Anthony 32, 33, 46
Boym, Svetlana 14, 109, 137

Bright Knight 32, 39, 41, 44, 45, 135
Brooker, Will 18, 20, 24, 32, 35, 37, 109, 110, 111, 137, 139
Brown, Jeffrey A. 22, 35, 41, 43, 44, 137
Burke, Liam 110, 137
Burton, Tim viii, 2–3, 12, 47, 49–50, 54, 58, 60–8, 70, 75–7, 84, 95–6, 98, 100–1, 103–5, 108–9, 114, 116, 118, 121, 124, 138
Buscemi, Steve 100

Cage, Nicolas 56, 100
Camp Knight 13, 30, 32, 35, 36, 37, 38, 40, 41, 44, 45, 67, 76, 94
Carrey, Jim 2, 7, 10, 60, 68, 113, 127
Chandler, Raymond 91
Clooney, George 73, 91, 93, 95, 98, 99, 102, 121, 123, 124
Cohen, Michael 72, 137
Collinson, Gary 99, 137
Coolio 100
Crew, David 115
Cute Knight 13, 32, 41, 44, 45, 67, 94

Dad Knight 32, 39, 40, 41, 44, 45, 67, 94, 99, 123
Dark Knight viii, 6–7, 9–13, 17–19, 21–5, 27–37, 40, 42–9, 58–9, 67, 70, 74, 76, 79–80, 82, 87–8, 90–1, 93–5, 97, 99, 107–8, 110, 112, 118–19, 121–4, 126–7, 133–5, 137
De Vito, Danny 62, 66, 100
Deodato, Mike 89
Desris, Joe 35, 36, 89, 138
Detective Comics 9, 16, 17, 18, 19
Dick Tracy 72, 73, 137
Dini, Paul 100
Dixon, Chuck 92, 105
Dixon, Wheeler Winston 110, 137
Doctor Strange 29

Dondero, Jennifer 21, 29, 137
Douglas, Michael 55
Dozier, William 35, 37, 38
Dudenhoeffer, Larrie 94, 137
Durand, Kevin K. 25, 26, 137, 138

Eco, Umberto 28, 138
Edward Scissorhands 54, 62
Elfman, Danny 45, 75, 76
Eltell, Christian Colby 114, 127
Englund, Robert 100
Eury, Michael 41, 138

Falling Down 50, 51, 55
Farrell, Collin 56, 57
Feige, Kevin 1, 3, 4, 11, 15, 131, 132
Field, James 133, 138
Filmation 38, 39, 40, 46, 94
Final Fight 85
Fincher, David 52, 56
Finger, Bill 18, 24, 47
Fink, Richard 5, 6, 15
Fiske, John 20
Flash Gordon 41, 132
Flatliners 51, 53, 55
Fleming, Dan 41, 42, 79, 138
Fraga, Kristian 63, 138
Fraser, Greg 133
Friedenthal, Andrew 26, 28, 138

Garcia, Bob 35, 36, 138
Ghostbusters 38
G.I. Joe 42
Giacchino, Michael 133
Giger, Hans Rudolf 10
Gleiberman, Owen 50, 51, 103
Goldblatt, Stephen 70, 126
Goldblum, Jeff 100
Goldenthal, Elliott 60, 75, 76, 104
Goldsman, Akiva 7, 10, 15, 58, 70, 75, 114
Gough, Michael 14, 69, 98
Graham, Richard 110, 137
Grisham, John 58, 59
Gunn, James 131, 132, 134

Hall, Stuart 20
Hamilton, Edmond 17

Hamm, Sam 65
Hanley, Tim 78, 138
Hanna-Barbera 40
Hays, Matthew 52, 103
He-Man and the Masters of The Universe 38
Holmes, John 113, 127

Iron Man 1

Jackson, Samuel L. 59
Javins, Marie 131, 138
Jeffries, Dru 71, 138
Jenkins, Henry 108, 109, 139
Johnston, Jacob 132, 138
Jones, Kelley 90, 91
Jones, Tommy Lee 2, 73, 113
Jurassic Park 31

Kane, Bob 18, 24, 47
Kasem, Casey 39
Kaveney, Roz 110, 138
Keaton. Michael 30, 31, 67, 104, 121, 122
Kelly, R. 94, 95
Kemp, Jan 36, 37
Kenner 42, 44, 66, 79, 80, 81, 104, 117
Kidman, Nicole 9, 56, 69, 122
Kilmer, Val 10, 11, 73, 82, 93, 95, 96, 99, 102, 114, 115, 121, 122, 123, 128
Kirby, Jack 132
Klock, Geoff 91, 92, 138
Kukkonen, Karin 26, 27, 138

Lee, Jim 89
Legends of Batman 42, 43
Lego Batman 29, 30, 31
Liefeld, Rob 89
Ling, Barbara 69, 126
Lite Knight 77, 87, 102
Loeb, Jeph 91
Love, Courtney 100
Lund, Anthony 8, 15

Madonna 100
Mamatas, Nick 45, 138
Martinson, Leslie H. 38
McCloud, Scott 71, 138

McConaughey, Matthew 59
McFarlane, Todd 89
McGregor, Ewan 100
McRobbie, Angela 20
Miller, Frank 19, 22, 48, 49, 91
Moench, Doug 90, 91
Moldoff, Sheldon 17, 19, 48
Morley, David 20
Morrison, Grant 19, 20, 46
Mortal Kombat 86, 87
Morton, Drew 29, 37, 71, 138
Mother Goose 42
Mulvey, Laura 89

Neill, Ve 69
Neon Knight viii–ix, 13, 17, 30, 32, 35, 41, 45, 47, 60, 67, 73–4, 76, 78, 80–1, 83, 87, 90–1, 94, 99, 101–2, 107, 111–12, 115–24, 126–7, 133–5
Nicholson, Jack 66, 100
Nightmare Before Christmas 63
Ninja Gaiden 85, 86
Nolan, Christopher 12, 33, 47, 119, 131, 133
Nolan, Graham 92

O'Donnell, Chris 10
O'Neil, Tegan 53, 74, 103, 104, 106
Ong, Walter 28, 30
Owczarski, Kimberly Ann 70, 71, 138

Pagnucci, Gian S. 24, 139
Pearson, Roberta E. 20, 23, 24, 32, 35, 138, 139
Peretti, Daniel 32, 139
Perry, Frank 49
Pfeiffer, Michelle 62, 66
Phone Booth 50, 55
Prescott, Norm 38
Proctor, William 27, 139
Protosevich, Mark 99, 100, 101
Pumphrey, Nicholaus 30, 139
Puzo, Mario 91

Raimi, Sam 4
Raynor, Max 9
Reeves, George 92
Reeves, Matt 116, 119, 133, 134

Reinhart, Mark S. 34, 37, 61, 63, 64, 66, 70, 139
Rickatson, Neil ix, 117
Robinson, James 90
Robinson, Jerry 18
Rodgers, Will 39, 40, 139
Romagnoli, Alex S. 24, 139
Rose, Charlie 31, 57, 59
Ross, Alex 91
Roussos, Eleni 132, 139

Sale, Tim 91
Scheimer, Lou 38
Schumacher, Joel viii–ix, 1–10, 12–15, 30–2, 34–5, 42–3, 45–61, 63, 67–78, 80–3, 87–107, 109–22, 124–9, 131–6
Schwarzenegger, Arnold 68, 73, 91
Scivally, Bruce 93, 139
Scott, Ridley 18
Seal 94
Semple Jr., Lorenzo 35
Seven 52, 56
Shazam! 39
Short, Martin 100
Silvestri, Alan 76
Singer, Bryan 4
Singer, Michael 62, 68, 69, 70, 139
Slaski, Danny 65
Smashing Pumpkins 94
Snyder, Zack 8, 22, 71
Sontag, Susan 35
Soule, Olan 39
Spider-Man 1, 4
Spigel, Lynn 108, 139
Sprang, Dick 48
Star Trek: The Animated Series 38
Starlin, Jim 132
Sutherland, Hal 38
Swenson, Robert 'Jeep' 92, 93

Tamaki, Mariko 9
Teenage Mutant Ninja Turtles 90
The Adventures of Batman 38, 39, 40
The Adventures of Superboy 38
The Batman 116, 119, 133, 134, 136, 138, 139
The Batman/Tarzan Adventure Hour 39
The Brave and the Bold 19, 22, 29

The Dark Knight Returns 22, 24, 48, 91
The Hardy Boys 38
The Incredible Shrinking Woman 51, 54, 55
The Lost Boys 50, 52, 55
The New Adventures of Batman 39
The New Adventures of Superman 39
The Phantom of the Opera 51
The Superman/Aquaman Hour of Adventure 39
Thor: Love & Thunder 3, 6, 134
Thor: Ragnarok 5, 6, 131, 132, 139
Thurman, Uma 80, 92, 113
Tibbetts, John C. 77, 104
Tigerland 50, 51, 52, 56, 57, 102
Timm, Bruce 100
Tomlin, Lily 54
Transformers 42
Trespass 56

U2 94
Urichio, William 20, 23, 24, 32, 35, 138, 139

Veronica Guerin 52, 55

Wai, Wong-Kar 132
Waid, Mark 91
Waititi, Taika 3, 6, 134
Wan, James 132
Wandtke, Terrence R. 27, 30, 139
Waters, Daniel 65
Watkiss, John 90
Weldon, Glen 35, 61, 62, 111, 139
Wertham, Fredric 37
West, Adam viii, 2, 12, 30, 31, 35, 38, 39, 40, 41, 49, 108
West, William 42
Willems, Patrick H. 30, 31, 46, 47
Williams, John 76
Williams, Paul 20
Williamson, Al 132
Wilson, Lewis 47
Wood, Dave 19
Woollacot, Janet 20, 137
World's Finest 21
Wright, Edgar 71

X-Men 1, 4, 89

Yan, Cathy 3
Young, Matthew David 76, 139

Zack Snyder's Justice League 8

www.ingramcontent.com/pod-product-compliance
Lightning Source LLC
Chambersburg PA
CBHW052051300426
44117CB00012B/2068